SEALS' FAMILY PRAISE FOR
AMONG HEROES

"This is more than a collection of stories about eight SEALs who gave their lives for their country. It also shows us the humanity of each of these men—the ordinary within the extraordinary, and a level of dedication and devotion we can strive to exemplify in our own lives."

—Jack Scott, father of Dave Scott

"I know now that I'm not alone in carrying Dave in my heart, my mind, my soul, and that gives me great comfort. Because, despite the enormous cavern I've carved out for him in my heart, I know it isn't enough to contain all of him; it will take more hearts than mine alone."

—Kat Colvert, widow of Dave Scott

"To his family, Matthew was *always* a person worthy of emulating. It's a comforting and inspiring thing for us to know that others feel the same way too."

—Donna Axelson, mother of Matt Axelson

"Thank you, Brandon and John, for sharing Glen's story. His sacrifice left a huge hole in the hearts of all who loved him. We hope he will continue to inspire others to live large."

—Katie Quigley, sister of Glen Doherty

"I am honored that John's story, and all these great men's stories, have been preserved not only for our children and grandchildren but for future generations of all Americans."

—Jackie Zinn, widow of John Zinn

continued . . .

"The war has taken so much from so many of us, and making the transition from grieving Chris's death to celebrating his life has been a painful process. You have blessed us by capturing the personality of the amazing man who graced our family for almost thirty-seven years."

—Cindy Campbell, sister of Chris Campbell

"*Among Heroes* hits the common thread among all these fine young men. Mikey wasn't a superman; he was entirely human. It's just that these guys were willing to give the last spark inside themselves to protect each other and their country, or die trying."

—Michael Bearden Sr., father of Mike Bearden

AMONG HEROES

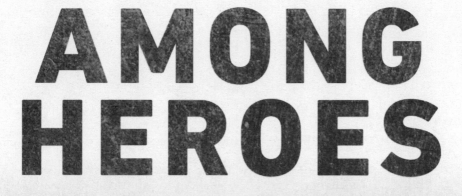

A U.S. NAVY SEAL'S TRUE STORY OF FRIENDSHIP, HEROISM, AND THE ULTIMATE SACRIFICE

BRANDON WEBB

with JOHN DAVID MANN

NAL
CALIBER

NAL CALIBER
Published by New American Library,
an imprint of Penguin Random House LLC
375 Hudson Street, New York, New York 10014

This book is a publication of New American Library. Previously published in an NAL Caliber hardcover edition.

First NAL Caliber Trade Paperback Printing, May 2016

For more information about Penguin Random House, visit penguin.com.

NAL CALIBER TRADE PAPERBACK ISBN: 978-0-451-47563-3

THE LIBRARY OF CONGRESS HAS CATALOGED THE HARDCOVER EDITION OF THIS TITLE AS FOLLOWS:
Webb, Brandon.
Among heroes: a U.S. Navy SEAL's true story of friendship, heroism, and the ultimate sacrifice/ Brandon Webb with John David Mann.
p.   cm.
ISBN 978-0-451-47562-6
1. United States. Navy. SEALs—Biography.   2. Special operations (Military science)—United States—History—21st century.   I. Mann, John David.   II. Title.   III. Title: a U.S. Navy SEAL's true story of friendship, heroism, and the ultimate sacrifice.
VG87.W428   2015
359.0092'273—dc23   2014032399

Printed in the United States of America
10 9 8 7 6 5 4 3 2 1

Designed by Spring Hoteling

PUBLISHER'S NOTE
While the author has made every effort to provide accurate telephone numbers and Internet addresses at the time of publication, neither the publisher nor the author assumes any responsibility for errors, or for changes that occur after publication. Further, publisher does not have any control over and does not assume any responsibility for author or third-party Web sites or their content.

Penguin
Random
House

To the families

In thinking back on the days of Easy Company, I'm treasuring my remark to a grandson who asked, "Grandpa, were you a hero in the war?"

"No," I answered, "but I served in a company of heroes."

—Mike Ranney, in *Band of Brothers*,
by Stephen E. Ambrose

AUTHOR'S NOTE

All the events in this book are true and are described herein to the best of my recollection. The names of the heroes in this book are real; however, some connected names have been changed to protect the identities of people incidental to these stories and of friends who are still in active duty. I have at all times sought to avoid disclosing particular methods and other sensitive mission-related information, and this book was submitted to the Department of Defense for a full review prior to publication. As much as possible, stories of my friends and their exploits have been compiled in full collaboration and partnership with family members.

CONTENTS

AMONG HEROES

INTRODUCTION

When I joined the Navy in 1993 I was a fresh-faced kid, barely out of high school. Like most nineteen-year-olds, I thought I knew something of the world. I had no inkling of the struggles that lay ahead.

Nor did much of the country. The America of 1993 was a world quite different from what it is today. The Cold War was over, the Soviet Union collapsed under the weight of its own obsolescence, and the deadly malaise now known as the Global War on Terror barely a blip on the horizon. Nestled in its valley between those two epochs of global conflict, the 1990s seemed a golden age of peace and prosperity. In many ways it was a time of fantasy and naïveté, and it would not last long. In the first light of the twenty-first century's dawning we would awaken to stark geopolitical realities. The very nature of war would radically change, and my friends and I would be on the front lines of the new warfare.

These were also the years of my passage from swaggering teen years to a more sober, reflective adulthood. On the way I would make a solid handful of the best friends in the world. Many of them I would soon lose.

It's a strange place I find myself in these days. When I talk with people in their eighties or nineties, they describe what it's like seeing so many of their friends vanish, one by one, and finding themselves progressively more alone in the world. That's a normal part of the cycle of life, I know—but I've been having that experience for years, and I'm barely forty.

The U.S. Special Operations community is one of the fiercest and most experienced fighting forces the world has ever seen. But we have been at war now for well over a decade, the longest continuous state of armed conflict in our history as a nation. This has put an enormous stress on all men and women in uniform, along with their families and friends. Given the unique nature of today's asymmetrical warfare, it has placed an especially heavy burden on our Special Operations community. Many of my closest friends in the SEAL teams are no longer here. They sacrificed everything, many leaving behind mothers, fathers, wives, and children.

At the same time, they also left behind powerfully instructive examples of living—models of what it means to be a hero.

This is the story of eight heroes whose lives intersected with mine during those years, men who gave their lives for their country and their team. Men who gave pieces of themselves to me, and without whom I would not be the man I am today. I trained with them and fought with them, looked up to them and learned from them. I miss them all terribly, yet at the same time, they're here with me still.

"Leave no man behind" is the mantra of all Special Operations teams. The purpose of this book is to help ensure that these eight heroes are not left behind. Within these stories of friendship and character you'll find the principles that guided these men in their lives, principles I have adopted in my own life and share with my children. Knowing these great men—who they were, how they lived, and what they stood for—has changed my life. We can't let them be forgotten.

So read about these amazing men, share their stories, and learn from them as I have. We've mourned their deaths. Let's celebrate their lives.

—Brandon Webb

1

SUPERHERO

MIKE BEARDEN

I t was still early, maybe one o'clock in the afternoon, and already creeping into the low nineties. It would get hotter still, we knew that for certain. Late spring in California's Central Valley, dry and brown, a clear day, the barometer high and steady, but to us the atmospheric pressure felt like roughly ten thousand pounds per square inch.

My best friend, Glen Doherty, and I were crouched down side by side at the front of a thousand-yard high-power shooting lane, on the last day of the marksmanship phase of the Naval Special Warfare Sniper School, arguably the toughest military training program on the planet. We were about to start our final test of this phase, the test that would determine whether we went on through the rest of the school or returned home in defeat. We'd been here for six weeks. A third of the class had already washed out, and we were terrified that we were next.

The idea of sniper school probably sounds romantic, exciting, adventurous. It's none of those things. It's fucking miserable. We would come back to our tents at the end of every interminable twelve-hour day dirty as hell, beaten down, exhausted, and already feeling the crushing weight of what loomed ahead of us the next day.

That pressure is mostly mental. Of course you have to be in top physical condition, but we were all SEALs. Physically, we'd already had "normal" redefined for us and the bar set insanely high. But sniper school was not about sheer physical endurance. It was about absorbing complex skill sets and executing them flawlessly, at a machine-gun pace, and under conditions of constantly increasing intensity. Seven days a week, twelve hours a day, we were *always* on—up at six a.m. to run out onto the range with rifle in hand and a single round, which we had to fire with sleep-stiffened fingers through still-cold rifle barrels at whatever moment they told us, at whatever target they told us, and hit it. Miss that early-morning shot and the rest of the day would feel like one long battle to regain any sense of confidence and morale. It was the most exacting, focused state of concentration any of us in the course had ever experienced. We were the proverbial frog in the pot of water being steadily brought to a boil, and the only way out of the pot was to fail.

Which was exactly what many of our classmates had done. In the weeks leading up to this test, some guys had come unglued under the strain and ended up fighting with their shooting partners. By "fighting" I don't mean "exchanging heated words"; I mean punching, mashing, and kicking, the kind of brawl you have to wade into and physically pull apart if you don't want too many broken bones.

What made the pressure worse for Glen and me was that we were both still new guys. In the SEAL teams, "new guys" are SEALs who have made it through BUD/S but have not yet done a full year–plus specialized training workup and gone on an overseas deployment. A new guy's job is pretty simple: Shut up and listen. Do what you're told. Be invisible and act like you don't know anything, because the truth is, you don't. Naval Special Warfare (NSW) Sniper School has a global reputation; even within the teams it is the most respected school of them all. The idea of a couple of new guys having the privilege of attending sniper school was more than some could take.

Especially the instructor hovering over Glen and me right now as we inched through the ordeal of our final test. This guy, a genuinely nasty turd named Slattery, hated our guts. He *wanted* us to fail.

And he happened to be the one grading us today.

As Slattery bitched at us, the day continued creeping forward on its belly toward the hottest part of the afternoon, the rising temperature not only adding to our stress but also physically affecting our test conditions. As metal heats up it expands. That produces an increase in pressure on the bullet as it traverses the interior of the swelling rifle barrel, which in turn increases the round's speed and alters the arc of its trajectory. As the mercury rose out on the California range, the increasing temperature differentials threading through the bone-dry foothills around us also caused the sporadic gusts of wind to intensify. Which put every critical factor in our environment in flux, increasing the difficulty level of our task to an insane degree.

In the field, your life often depends on making the shot. Out here on the range, it was just our careers on the line.

At this point Glen and I had completed the "snaps and movers" portion of the test. Snaps and movers involves targets that suddenly pop up out of nowhere at unpredictable time intervals (snaps), and others that slide continuously right and left in random and unpredictable patterns and speeds (movers). Now we were in the second portion, called UKD, or unknown distances, which employed targets of variable range and elevation, none of this communicated to us. In snaps and movers we at least knew how far away our targets were. Not in UKD. For this portion of the test the spotter had to employ complex observations and calculations, using the mil dot reticle in his scope (two tiny lines of illuminated dots arranged like crosshairs) to determine exactly how far away that damn thing was. And we weren't using handheld computers, like we do these days in the field. We had to do all that math by hand, with the seconds ticking away.

I was shooting first, Glen reading the conditions, calling wind and elevation, and keeping track of our time. We had to move through a course with multiple lanes and multiple shots within a precise given time frame. Which meant a hell of a lot of calculation, preparation, and execution had to happen every sixty seconds without fail. We'd cleared two lanes and were setting up for the final shot on our third. As I focused on the image in my scope, time slowed to a crawl. Glen was taking it slow and careful, working to read the shifting wind currents.

Something felt wrong. We were taking too long. "How much time?" I muttered.

"We're good," I heard him murmur back. "Plenty of time."

I felt my breath flow out and waited for that moment of complete neutrality that hangs motionless between exhale and inhale, the instant of maximum focus and minimum body interference, gently increasing my finger pressure on the trigger pull—

"Time!"

I whipped a look over toward that asswipe Slattery and saw a triumphant leer on his ugly puss. He was holding up his timepiece in one hand, like he'd just picked an especially big booger he was proud of and wanted to show his ma.

"Time, gentlemen," he repeated, savoring the moment.

My heart stopped. What the *fucking hell*?

Not only had I not taken the shot, but we still had two more lanes and eight rounds to go. Something had gone wrong with Glen's timepiece. We had fucked up.

"You guys are screwed," Slattery crowed. "Good luck coming back from that one. You dipshits are going home."

He was right: Coming back from this disaster would be close to impossible. In order to make up for all the shots I'd just failed to take and survive the test, Glen would now have to score no less than a 95 on his five lanes. Out of twenty shots, in other words, he could a miss a maximum of one. Any more than that and I'd be going home, and Glen might be, too, because in those days shooter-spotter teams were graded together.

And shooting a 95 on this range was an extremely rare occurrence.

I could see that Glen was much worse off than me. I was only freaked out. He didn't utter a word, but he was obviously devastated. *Oh, my God*, his expression said, *I just fucked you over.*

"Look, dude." I spoke quickly and quietly so Slattery wouldn't hear. "It's behind us. Forget it. We have to clean this thing's clock. Let's just shoot a hundred and move on."

This was something sniper school taught me: no regrets. You can't focus on the shot you just took. Once it's out of the barrel, you'll never get it back. And it's not true just on the rifle. It's true in any situation—every action, every word, every thought. It's over. Move on. Assess, adjust, improve, and make the next one count.

We got to work, me calculating and calling every shot and Glen nailing it. In the first lane, the one with the closest targets, I heard four *pings* in succession as Glen aced four shots out of four. We moved on to lane two and he did the same thing, and again in lane three, and yet again in lane four. Now we were in lane five, shooting out to unknown distances up to a thousand yards on the big bolt-action .300 Winchester Magnum. The .300 Win Mag bullet doesn't go subsonic until somewhere between 1,350 and 1,400 yards, which meant it would be traveling at well beyond the speed of sound all the way from the instant of ignition to the instant of impact. I called the shot, and Glen took it. The lead slug flew out to meet the steel silhouette—and I heard no *ping*. Nothing. The round had harmlessly passed the target by.

There it was: our one miss. One more and I was out.

Slattery audibly snickered and muttered something we both willed ourselves not to hear. We were busy.

Calculating your round's flight path *before* the shot is only the first part of the spotter's job. The next task is to follow the vapor trail the round leaves in its wake as it pierces the air, called its *trace*. I had followed that bullet's trace the way a hawk tracks the path of a chipmunk dashing across a field for the safety of the forest. I'd seen exactly where it went, and I murmured an instantaneous course correction in Glen's ear.

Ping . . . ping . . . ping—he hit the remaining three shots with clean precision. We were finished. I was safe.

We all stood around as they read off everyone's score. Glen's implausible nineteen out of twenty had given him a personal tally of 95, which not only had saved my ass but also was the highest score for the day. Except for one thing: As far-fetched as it sounded, another new guy in the class had shot a 95, too.

Which meant the day's shooting was not over yet.

Someone had donated a beautiful SKS 7.62 semiautomatic rifle to the class. This thing was a work of art, a classic Soviet-made carbine (this was the service rifle that preceded the AK-47), and a piece any gun owner would be proud to have in his collection. Before our test that day the instructors had told us that whoever came out with the highest score would go home with that rifle. But you can't exactly saw an SKS in half, so now Glen and the other guy were going to stage a shoot-off.

This time these guys would each be on their own, no shooter-spotter teams. Each shooter would have just a few minutes to do all his own spotting, calculations, wind call, and the rest, then get one shot—and only one shot—at that lane's target. They would take turns, starting at the closest distance and ending at a thousand yards.

The rest of us huddled around, cheering on our favorite horse, me the loudest voice in the Glen camp.

In the first lane, both shooters nailed their targets. And the second, and the third, and the fourth. It was an electric experience, quietly watching the execution of perfection. These guys were both phenomenal shots.

On the fifth and final target, Glen sighted the thousand-yard distance and got himself ready, slowly squeezed the trigger . . . and missed. A groan went up in the crowd.

The other guy got down in the dirt, went through his preparations, squeezed—and also missed. Another groan went up, laced with laughter, catcalls, and the usual volley of insults and obscenities. SEALs are not known to be overly tender with one another's feelings.

Glen lay down in the lane again, took his second shot . . . and missed once more.

The other guy hit it square.

Predictably, a roar went up, and we all grabbed the guy and started pounding on him in congratulation. The SKS was his, but victory belonged to all of us, as we stampeded off the range in a raucous mass to go track down adult beverages in large quantities. It was a heady moment. The shooting portion of the class was over, and we'd survived it. Even though my best friend had lost the contest, I really didn't care, and neither did Glen. For one thing, we were both so relieved just to have passed the damn course.

But there was another reason we didn't care. If anyone else had beaten Glen, we probably would have been at least a *little* ticked off. SEALs are over-the-top competitive, and Glen even more so than most. But it happened that the shooter who had edged Glen out and taken possession of that SKS was such a likable guy, so universally loved and respected, it was impossible to feel anything but happy that he'd won.

His name was Mike Bearden. They called him the Bear.

I first met Bearden two years earlier, in the summer of 1998. We were all fresh from BUD/S, the legendary seven-month training program that all SEAL candidates undergo and only a fraction complete. Except that's a misnomer: BUD/S isn't really *training*; it's more like a seven-month entrance exam. What we were doing now in the summer of '98, *this* was training. SEAL tactical training, or STT, was what happened to those who made it *through* BUD/S and came out the other end still standing. Over the three months of STT (these days it's called SEAL qualification training, or SQT), we had drilled into us weapons skills, close-quarters battle tactics and coordinated room-to-room takedown, advanced land navigation and survival, extended dives and underwater demolition, and desert warfare. For this last, they took us to the Niland desert, one of the strangest places I've ever seen.

Along the edge of the Salton Sea, a huge, strongly alkaline runoff lake that lurks well below sea level at roughly the same elevation as Death Valley, the Niland desert is a vast stretch of lunar landscape in the wishfully named Imperial Valley, where the central Californian desert bleeds out to the Mexican border. Niland makes an excellent surrogate Middle Eastern battleground. Most of *Jarhead* and the sand dune sequences in *Independence Day* and *Star Wars* were filmed there. Great place to prepare for war in Iraq or Afghanistan—although we were still a few years away from knowing that was what we were doing.

Toward the end of our time at Niland, one of our instructors decided that, because the 75th Ranger Regiment (the Army's Spec Ops guys) were doing a twelve-mile forced march as part of their course, we needed to do that, too. "Hell, we're frogmen," went the thinking. "If they can do it, we sure as shit can do it better." Instead of twelve miles, he figured, we'd make it fourteen.

Which was fine, except for two things. First, the Rangers didn't just wake up one day and do a twelve-mile loaded march. They built up to it throughout their training. Also there was no room in our existing schedule to slip in an exercise like that. No worries: This guy figured he would just tack it onto the end of a full day of training. Like a P.S. on a letter. A really long, really heavy P.S.

So here we were on a fourteen-mile forced run, with full gear (including fifty-pound ruck), on an evening after we'd already done a five-hour land nav course that day from noon till five. In the middle of the desert. In July. And we had to do it in three hours. Out of seventy-two guys, only four made it under the three-hour gun. Barely another dozen of us made it back at all. The rest of the guys were strewn over the fourteen-mile course, and corpsmen (medics) had to haul them in. Some of them plain passed out. We used every IV in the camp that night.

And Bearden? He just crushed it. It hadn't even taken him that much effort.

All seventy-two of us knew what perseverance and focus were all about. We were SEALs, after all, which meant we were all maniacs to some degree. But the Bear was in a class by himself. As I watched him sauntering into quarters that evening, while dozens of our teammates were still getting IVs or draped near-comatose over their beds, I had this thought:

This guy is indestructible.

Mike Bearden had been through BUD/S just a few months before me, in Class 213. I had gone on to SEAL Team Three, while Mike went to Team Five. At Team Five the other guys called him the Commander, in part because he loved James Bond flicks. But it was that other nickname that stuck.

The Bear.

It wasn't just that those were the first four letters of his last name. The guy *looked* like a bear. The joke about Mike Bearden was that "everyone else looked up to him." The guy was enormous. But his height wasn't the only reason we all looked up to him. There was something distinctive about Mike, a commanding presence that made everyone around him feel safer because he was there. While he never grabbed the spotlight, he was the kind of guy all eyes turned to when he walked into the room. And it wasn't simply because he was huge. Mike carried himself with a sort of quiet dignity. He seemed somehow exempt from all the pushing and shoving. In a community where bragging is like breathing, he never talked about himself, and he never trash-talked anyone else, either. I never heard him bitch or complain, not about anything, not once. He just went about his business and got the job done.

Mike apparently had some sort of alchemy going on there, because he could make friends with anyone. It wasn't as if he went out of his way to do that. It just seemed effortless. Once when he was in high school (as I later learned), Mike tackled an all-star fullback for the opposing team and hit him so hard he tore up the guy's ankle. So what happened? The two became best friends. Before long Mike was going out with a girl who also happened to be very close friends with this same fullback whose ankle Mike had messed up. All three of them became close friends, and they stayed that way. The girl's name was Derenda Henderson. A few years later it changed to Derenda Bearden. Classic Mike: wreck a guy's ankle, become his best bud and marry his close friend, and everyone's happy.

Mike was the guy who would take time out to help someone who was having trouble figuring out how to use some weapons system, or fill out some confusing piece of paperwork. He was everyone's big brother. And that quality intrigued me.

Growing up I'd been close to my little sister (my only sibling), but I'd never had a big brother, and my relationship with my dad was troubled. We moved fairly often as our family fortunes rose and fell, and each time I'd feel uprooted once again, forced to carve out new territory and new alliances, usually with a mix of wits and fists. I'd spent much of my teenage years on the docks of southern California, leaving home altogether by the age of sixteen. Throughout my childhood I'd been mostly concerned with looking out for myself. Mike Bearden seemed like he'd lived his whole life watching out for everyone else. To me this was both fascinating and inspiring. I wanted to be more like Mike.

I needed to understand what made him tick.

When Mike was just one year old his family moved to the Houston area so that Mike's dad, Michael Senior, could pursue a doctorate in education there. To support the family, Mike's parents, Michael and Peggy, needed to scare up some income as well as a place to stay. Michael Senior had worked as a teacher, and Peggy had child-care experience, so they took a position running a home for 144 abused and abandoned children, a career they continued for the next two decades. Which meant that Mike and his three siblings grew up in a home together with dozens of kids who had been rescued out of situations ranging from bad to unthinkably bad, an experience that bred into the Bearden children a bone-deep sense of compassion for the downtrodden.

Sometimes on Sunday afternoons, during court-appointed visitation periods, some of the home residents would receive visits from parents or other relatives. Then there were those kids who, after looking forward to the visit all week, would simply sit and wait for a parent who never showed. Mike and his older sister, Wendy, would sit with them, wordlessly feeling their pain. It made an impression Mike never forgot.

No wonder the guy felt like everyone's big brother when we were in the teams together. That was pretty much who he *was*.

And then there was that business of his indomitable spirit. As a kid, according to his parents, Mike was always determined to get into the game. Michael Senior had coached high school football while working his way through his undergrad degree, and now, to help give these disadvantaged kids as normal a life as possible, he started an athletic team for the boys, and Peggy started a team for the girls. Mike loved sports and would tag along with his dad to all their ball games.

When Mike was eight, the Bearden team was playing a visiting team from Austin. Bearden Senior had turned away from the field to take care of something on the sidelines that needed his attention, when suddenly a shout went up and a wave of laughter rippled through the crowd. He looked up and realized that everyone was yelling and pointing at something going on out on the field.

Oh, boy, he thought, *what now?* He strode out onto the field and sure enough, there was little Mike smack in the middle of the action. He had sneaked off into the locker room, wriggled into a full uniform, and run out onto the field to get into the game. The fact that the team jersey hung down around his knees like a dress didn't seem to bother him a bit. He had his game face on. He was out there to play some ball.

When Mike was twelve he announced that he wanted to run a marathon. "You can't run a marathon," his dad told him. "You're just starting seventh grade."

"No, I'm gonna run," he insisted. "Look right here." He pointed to an announcement in the newspaper for the Houston marathon. His dad offered a compromise: They would take him to *watch* the race that year. "No," repeated Mike, "I'm gonna *run* in it."

Somehow he talked his dad into it, and when the day came, there was Mike out on the starting line, wearing his running shoes and his number on the back of his shirt. His parents figured he'd run a block or two and then quit when he realized just how outclassed he was. But "outclassed" was a foreign concept to Mike, then and always. When the gun went off he took off, too, and he didn't stop. About half an hour later the Beardens heard an ambulance siren starting up. They looked at each other and shook their heads. Ten minutes later the ambulance returned with its twelve-year-old passenger. Mike had run that marathon until he collapsed in the street.

No matter what the sport, Mike wanted to get in there and carry the team on his shoulders. The problem was, he just wasn't all that big—and by this time he was impatient to get growing. At his annual physical when he was eleven, the year before his marathon, he asked the family pediatrician, "Doc, you think I'll ever grow? Am I always going to be this little?"

"Well, Mike," the doctor said, "would you rather be tall, or would you rather be smart?"

That didn't stop Mike for a second. "I want to be both!" he shot back.

Meanwhile, if he couldn't be tall, he could make up for it by climbing up onto tall places. Which he did, constantly. Every chance he got to climb something and jump off, he took it—climbing trees, scaling walls, scurrying up statues, anything. One day when his parents were out, he invited all his friends to come over and swim in the pool they had on their property, which was situated right next to a good-size gymnasium they used for the children's exercise and athletics. The Beardens later found out that while the other kids swam, Mike spent the afternoon climbing up on the roof of the gym and diving off into the pool.

As a boy Mike was a huge fan of comic-book superheroes. He had a Superman T-shirt with a big red S on it that he loved to wear around the property. Of course, that wasn't unusual. A lot of kids his age had fantasies about being a superhero when they grew up. But Mike was serious about it. Firefighters captured his imagination. He could think of nothing more exciting than climbing up into a burning building, rescuing someone, and jumping out with them to safety.

He was never one to pick a fight or go looking for trouble, and when arguments came up he would play the diplomat and try to persuade everyone to get along. But he didn't like bullies, and he refused to stand by and let anyone pick on anyone else. Through his school years his teachers routinely pointed out that little Mike was someone who always stood up for the underdog.

One year, when he was in Scotland on tour with his church choir, Mike's parents got a transatlantic call from the choir director. *Uh-oh*, they thought when they learned who was calling. *What now?* There was no problem, the choir director hastened to assure them; he just wanted to let them know what had happened. They'd all been walking around town that day as a group, and they happened to witness someone stealing something. Everyone else stood riveted to the spot and stared. As any true superhero would, Mike sprang into action, chased the guy down, and put a hammer-lock on him.

In the middle of Mike's fourteenth year, it finally happened: He starting growing . . . and kept on growing. His parents struggled to keep him in jeans that year, and the next, and the year after that. Before long he was six-foot-four, a lean, powerful 220 pounds, and the school's star athlete.

From Little League on through high school, Mike had gotten into every sport he could, and he excelled in all of them. He was an all-star catcher, a valued linebacker, and a star swimmer. One year his high school football team was running an undefeated season, leading their district with one of the highest scores in the state. In a run-up to the state championship they lost a coin flip and had to play a preliminary game to qualify. Mike was the starting fullback in that game and scored all his team's touchdowns. Two games earlier he had injured his knee and it had not fully recovered. Still, he played on. The two teams were neck-and-neck right down to the closing seconds, when the other team kicked a field goal and took the game by a point.

By the time he finished high school, Mike's knee was pretty bad. For his last four games he had to stop in at the doctor's office before each game to have the knee drained. The doc told him he shouldn't be playing ball at all, but he was determined, and when Mike was determined, that was that. His knee might be suffering, but so what? He was Captain Indestructible.

After graduating from high school, Mike spent a few years working out what exactly he wanted to do with his life. After a year of college he took a job as an assistant coach at Derenda's old high school, where he had the chance to accomplish as a coach the goal he had come so close to achieving as a quarterback: His undefeated team went right to the top and took the state championship that year. But as much as Mike loved coaching and loved football, he knew that wasn't what he was here to do with his life. He was here to save people. He didn't want to be a coach.

He wanted to be a superhero.

At the high school where he coached there was a picture in the school trophy case of a graduate who had gone on to become a SEAL. Mike was taken with it and started asking around, talking to anyone and everyone who had known that kid to find out whatever he could about him. One night not long after that his dad got a call.

"Dad," said Mike as soon as his father picked up. "I know what I want to do."

. . .

After STT I went on to my eighteen-month training workup with Team Three, and the Bear went on to train with Team Five, so we didn't see each other much for the next two years, until we both showed up in Coronado for our initial sniper school briefing in April of 2000. It was in the crucible of sniper school that we became closer friends, right up to the day he beat Glen in their shoot-off for that SKS rifle.

From our six weeks of marksmanship training up in Central Valley we caravanned back downstate to the scorching Martian landscape at Niland to see who would make it through the next portion of the course. Of the original twenty-six, there were now about eighteen of us left. By the end of the course only a dozen would graduate.

Shooting is one thing. Being able to get close enough to take the shot—and with such complete stealth that you can extract again without being captured, blown up, or shot yourself—is a whole other aspect of the sniper's craft.

In fact, while most people equate *sniper* with marksmanship, the truth is that the art of stalking—the ability to move about undetected while observing every aspect and detail of an environment—comes into play far more than the ability to place a well-directed kill shot. Make no mistake: When it's time to take that shot, it has to be perfect. (If you want to know just how crucial that is, just ask Captain Phillips of the *Maersk Alabama*.) But practically speaking, in the field we spend a lot more time in stalking and reconnaissance than we do shooting.

Picture a sniper stalking, and chances are good the images that come to mind have to do with a guy snaking along stealthily on his belly, or lying motionless for hours. Yes, those things happen. But that's not really what it's about. The lion's share of the skill of stalking, like that of shooting, is mental. The key is the ability to scan an entire environment and identify *dead space*, the three-dimensional area defined by a visual obstruction that can effectively shield you from an observer's view. In a way, the art of stalking comes down to the ability to make yourself invisible—not exactly a Jedi mind trick, but pretty close. And for some reason, getting the knack of this stalking mind-set was something that seemed to click for me and one other guy before it did for the rest of our classmates. By the last week of the course, I was far ahead enough in points that graduating was in the bag, and I stopped wearing my ghillie suit (a special stalking outfit we would customize with twigs and bits of vegetation) and began going out onto the course in my regular desert cammies just to confound and piss off the instructors.

Especially Slattery. (And yes, it *did* piss him off.)

Now, I am not a tall guy, and you might think being shorter was a major advantage in stalking. But it turned out size has nothing to do with it, and my proof for that assertion is Mike Bearden—who was the other guy in our class who clicked into the art of stalking right away.

It was an amazing thing to watch: this monster of a guy, and he could just make himself invisible. I'd be a few hundred yards into a stalk and pause to look around, and there'd be Mike, slipping along nearby like a wraith. And then there were all the other guys back near the start line, inching along frantically on their stomachs.

In our Navy training before BUD/S we all went through a school called SERE, an acronym for survival, evasion, resistance, and escape. Until I got to BUD/S, this school was the toughest damn training I'd ever had. At SERE they wanted to make sure you knew how to survive, whether on your own out in the wilderness or under conditions of hostile captivity, and they didn't pull any punches in the process.

I heard a story about Mike's time in SERE school. When it came to the evasion exercise, where students role-play escaped prisoners and try to avoid recapture, they couldn't find him. They'd rounded up all the other escapee-students, but even after scouring the entire area they couldn't find Bearden.

He had vanished.

Even after the evasion exercise was over, they *still* couldn't find him. The Bear, as the expression goes, was out in the woods. Finally they started combing the region in trucks, calling him in through loudspeakers. It turned out they couldn't find him because he had stayed hidden underwater, breathing through a reed. The Commander wasn't coming in till he was ready to come in.

On June 12, 2000, Mike, Glen, and I stood together with nine other classmates to receive our NSW Sniper School certificates. It was my twenty-sixth birthday; Mike was exactly twenty-seven years and three months old. His wife, Derenda, was there, along with their son, Holden, who was one day shy of nine months old. It was a proud time for all of us.

For most of us, deployment would be coming soon. First, though, Glen and I had a thirty-day leave coming, and we both took full advantage of it immediately after graduation.

For the Bear's part, he was moving right on to another school, this one involving one of his favorite activities: jumping from tall places. Mike was using this time to go through military freefall training right there in California.

Each of us had already been through rigger school, where you learn the basics of parachuting. There we had practiced a form of jumping called "static line," a whole row of us jumping together with our chutes automatically pulled for us, what we call "dope on a rope," and we'd also been through the exercise we call "hop-and-pops," where you jump out over water at a few thousand feet and pull immediately, World War II–style, like the American airborne landings in Normandy. A funny story from Mike's rigger-school days: While partying at someone's second-floor apartment after hours, Mike was sitting out on the balcony when he looked out and glimpsed a guy snatching a purse from a woman on the street below. He leaped off the balcony, landing on his feet, and went after the guy. Seeing this giant appearing out of the air and plowing toward him, the terrified thief took off down the street as fast as he could run, but he didn't have a chance. Just as he'd done on that high school choir trip in Scotland, Mike caught up with the perp and took him down with a flying tackle, then held him in a lock until the police showed up. That was Mike's version of basic jump training.

But this school Mike was going through now would take jumping to a whole different level. In military freefall he'd be jumping out of aircraft at ten to twelve thousand feet with full combat equipment. On an earlier visit to Coronado, his parents had seen some guys jumping out of a helicopter, and later that day Michael Senior had asked Mike, "How do you *do* that? I mean, you just throw yourself out of that thing. You don't hesitate."

Mike shrugged. "Hey, somebody's got to do it."

"But seriously," his dad persisted, "have you thought about how dangerous this all is?"

Mike said, "You know, Dad, I don't think about that. You *can't* think about that. This is our job. This is what we do. There are people out there who can't help themselves. Somebody's got to help them."

One day shortly after graduating from sniper school, Mike passed by the SEAL quarterdeck in Coronado on his way to get himself set up for jump school. A BUD/S instructor was finishing up with a group of fresh recruits, taking them through their punishing paces on the broiling-hot asphalt grinder. The instructor glanced up and spotted Mike walking by, recognizing him instantly. Reputation is everything in the SEAL teams, and everyone on the teams knew how well the new guys had done at sniper school, especially Mike.

"Hey, Bearden," the instructor called out. "Now that you've finished sniper school, what's next?"

Mike reached a fist up behind his neck and yanked, miming the action of opening a parachute. He grinned.

"I'm gonna be a sky god," he said.

A few weeks later, nearing the end of jump school, Mike drove himself, Derenda, and their infant son, Holden, the fifteen hundred miles home to eastern Texas to attend a cousin's wedding. The day after the wedding, he saddled the family up to head straight back out west so he could rejoin the class.

"Man," his dad said as Mike packed their bags, "I sure wish you could stay through the weekend. We could spend some time together."

"I can't, Daddy," said Mike. "We've got a jump coming up."

His dad nodded, said so long, and saw them off.

A few days later, on Tuesday evening, Mike called home to check in with his folks, as he was in the habit of doing. He told his dad he'd made a jump that day, and said his back was really sore. When you watch SEALs go through their paces in documentaries, it's easy to get the impression that we're invulnerable and nothing fazes us. The truth is, all that training takes its toll. Mike's knees had been dicey ever since high school, and while he never said a word about it to the other guys, they would hurt after jumping.

"Well," said his dad, "maybe you can skip tomorrow."

"Dad, you don't *skip*," Mike explained. "Besides, we're just about finished up here."

There was a pause in the conversation; then his dad said, "So, what are you going to do next, Mike?"

"What do you mean, what am I going to do next?" said Mike.

"Your four years are fixing to be up. Have you thought about what comes after this?"

Mike was silent for a moment before answering.

"Dad," he said, "I've found something worthwhile here. Yeah, I've had offers to go work for a few companies. And I've thought about working for the U.S. Marshals at some point. But for right now, I'm doing something I'm really good at."

Michael Senior digested that, then said, "So, what are you saying?"

"I'm going to re-up, Dad," Mike replied. "What we're doing here makes a *difference*. People need us."

"Okay," his dad said, and they said their good-byes.

It was the last time the two men spoke.

Michael Senior was at school teaching the next day, Wednesday, the twelfth of July, when someone came into the classroom and said he was needed at home right away. When he arrived home the news was waiting for him. That day the Bear had run smack into any military trainer's worst nightmare: His main chute had a rare malfunction and got tangled up in his secondary or backup chute, preventing the secondary from deploying.

He fought to the last second to get that canopy open—fought it all the way to the ground.

They held a funeral service for Mike Bearden on Wednesday, July 19, exactly one week after the freefall accident, at the First Baptist Church in Justin, Texas, the town where his wife's family lived. About twenty of Mike's teammates were there, flown out from the coast so they could be present for the service.

After the formal part of the service was over, little Holden looked over at my buddy Ed, who was a member of our sniper class, and pointed at his chest. Ed looked down. The boy's finger was pointing at the gold SEAL Trident pinned to his lapel. Holden recognized it, because his dad had one just like it. He looked up at Ed and said, "Hey, mister. Do you know where my dad is?"

Barely keeping his composure, Ed bent down and said, "He's in a better place, son." And then immediately felt like an ass. But what else could he say?

There were a lot of tears shed by some very tough SEALs

that day. Ed later told me it was the hardest thing he'd ever done, standing there in his dress blues as Mike's little boy kept asking the SEALs in uniform where his daddy was. "It was a fucking tear factory," is how he put it.

I wasn't there. In fact, I didn't even know Mike had died. I was fifteen hundred miles away, surfing off the California coast, oblivious to all of this. Immediately after graduating sniper school, I had gone on my thirty days' leave and had no idea what had happened. To tell the truth, though, even if I had known, I don't think I would have gone. I couldn't. It was too much.

Over the years to come, a lot of my teammates would die, but I wouldn't go to their funerals. It would be more than a decade before I would finally break down and attend a memorial service myself.

Mike's death shook us all up, and I took it hard. It was the first time I'd come face-to-face with the fact that death is an unavoidable part of what we do.

From the vantage point of today, so many years after 9/11, it's hard to remember what the world was like in July of 2000. In many ways, we in the United States were living in our own bubble. The Cold War had been over for a decade, and in terms of combat, there wasn't that much going on in the world. We'd lost four guys in Panama in '89, and had seen more than a dozen of our Spec Ops brothers slain in Mogadishu in '93, but those tragedies were brief and singular events that already seemed far removed in time. There was a sense of, if not exactly safety, at least relative calm, a sort of age of innocence. Yes, there were occasionally fatal accidents in training, but they were rare. We knew the life of a

SEAL was dangerous—at least, we knew it with our heads. But we didn't really expect to have to deal with the death of a comrade.

I'd been wrong. I'd seen Mike as indestructible. But he wasn't. None of us were.

When my friends and I were going through BUD/S a few years earlier, one of our instructors sat us down and told us, "Look around, gentlemen. Look at the guys on your left. Now look at the guys on your right. These are your teammates, your friends. And some of them are going to die. You're going to lose them. That's the way it is." *Yeah, yeah*, I remember thinking, *save the lecture and just let us get our four hours of sleep!* At the time his little speech had seemed melodramatic. Now it hit me that what he'd said was the simple truth. *They're your friends. And you're going to lose them.*

What made Mike's death all the more surreal was that it wasn't as if he had been killed on the battlefield. It would be easy to decry his loss as senseless. But that wasn't the truth. Tragic, yes. Wrenching, awful—absolutely. But not senseless.

The training we go through to become the most effective warriors possible is serious. It's not safe. Mistakes happen, because we're constantly stretching our limits. If we made the conditions of our training so safe that nobody could get hurt, the training would fail in its purpose. We have an expression in the teams: "The more you sweat in training, the less you bleed in combat." But it isn't just sweat. We bleed in training, too. We get pneumonia, break bones, and sometimes worse. The mortal dangers our Spec Ops guys face don't occur only in the cauldron of political hot spots around the world, but at every step along the way. Special Operations is a dangerous path, and those who tread it are putting everything on the line from day one. Mike died in the service of our country's safety and security—in other words, he died keeping *you and your family* safe—every bit as much as our friends who would die a few years later in the streets of Ramadi or the mountains of Afghanistan.

Mike died a hero's death. And we all were left to fight the survivor's battle: the one with shock, then anger and grief, and finally foreboding, knowing there were more losses to come. Because we all knew that death hadn't simply paid us a visit. It had come into our midst, staked its tent, taken up permanent residence. From this point on it would be our constant companion.

"You read war books, Clive Cussler and Richard Marcinko, things like that, and you get one kind of picture," Mike's dad told me years later. "But there's a human side to these guys you don't always read about. These are kids that mothers have brought into this world, and have raised and loved and held dear to their hearts, and you never dream that they're going to just lay down their lives for somebody else. But it makes you proud, too. They just see it as their job and don't think twice about it. Because if they didn't do it, who else would?"

It wasn't until several years after Mike's death, long after I'd been through the caves of Afghanistan and back, that I finally had the chance to go through my own military freefall training. Because of a fluke in scheduling, this had been the one piece of standard SEAL schooling that I hadn't managed to make. I'd been through the basic dope-on-a-rope stuff, but this was different. This was the jump Mike had been doing.

As I sat in that little twin-engine plane, feeling it climb to twelve thousand feet (an altitude sufficient to cause hypoxia if you're not wearing an oxygen mask) so we could throw ourselves out into the open sky, I felt a twinge of an emotion I wasn't accustomed to feeling.

Fear.

Mike's death had touched us all in a deep, dark place we don't often show or talk about. SEALs don't scare easily. Part of it is our training, and part of it is just who we are. To a degree every one of us on the teams shares that daredevil gene. But that doesn't mean we don't experience fear. We all have our own demons. Some guys have to conquer a fear of the water. In my case, Mike's death triggered a fear of skydiving, and now that fear was rising up like a dragon.

I told myself this was crazy. I loved flying. Since I was a kid I'd always aspired to become a pilot. I'd trained for this, and never for a moment thought I would have any hesitation when the time came to do it. But there it was.

One classmate saw that plane's rear ramp door open, sat himself right back down in his sideways-facing seat, and buckled himself in. "I'm done with this shit," he said, and he refused to jump. I knew how he felt. An expression we have in jump school flitted through my mind: *Why would you want to throw yourself out of a perfectly good airplane?* Guys say it as a joke to take the edge off the tension of the moment. Right then I wasn't seeing the humor in it. For a moment, I honestly didn't know if I could go through with it.

Then I thought about Mike. "What we're doing here makes a *difference*," he'd told his dad. "People need us." The fall may have killed his body, but I'd never forget that indestructible spirit.

I shook off the fear and jumped.

DAREDEVIL

DAVE SCOTT

On August 14, 2000, less than a month after Mike Bearden's funeral, my platoon took off westward across the Pacific on our first deployment, bound for the Indian Ocean as part of an amphibious readiness group (ARG) attached to the transport ship USS *Duluth*. Our days as new guys were finally coming to an end—and not one moment too soon. After years of training and preparation, we were so glad to be getting the hell out of Coronado, on our way to becoming seasoned operatives at last.

You'd think this would have been really exciting.

It wasn't.

For one thing, being part of an ARG was at the top of exactly nobody's list. As part of an ARG, we had weeks of being shipbound to look forward to. This was smart in an operational sense, but it sucked for us. Yes, SEALs are technically part of the Navy, but in practical fact we have nothing to do with the Navy per se, and the last thing we want to do is spend our time on a boat. Not only is it tedious as hell, but it's also practically impossible to stay in decent shape on a boat. Still, we gave it our all, putting in as much time as we could in the onboard gym lifting weights. On a ship, as they say, the acronym SEAL stands for Sleep, Eat, and Lift.

Even when we did get off the boat, there just wasn't all that much going on in the world. Trade sanctions against Saddam had been in place for a decade since Desert Storm, and as part of the multinational enforcement effort, SEAL teams were routinely involved in interdictions to curb the constant oil-smuggling traffic out of Iraq. That was an interesting gig, and we figured we would eventually have some fun doing ship boardings in the Gulf. But there wasn't any serious action happening anywhere.

We steamed southwest across the Pacific, with a few brief stops along the way at various exotic locations, until we reached the port town of Darwin, Australia, where we spent a week doing the things SEALs do to keep themselves occupied: joint training exercises with the Aussies, working out, and blowing off steam when we could. From there it was a quick hop north to war-torn East Timor, which had recently fought for its hard-won independence from Indonesia and was still in a shambles. A team of our guys went ashore for a few days to help in some humanitarian efforts there. And that was about as exciting as things got in those days. It was a time of unprecedented prosperity and stability, both in the States and in the world at large. To put it in SEAL terms, a pretty boring world.

That was about to change.

From East Timor we sailed westward through a series of stepping-stone stops—Singapore and Phuket, Thailand— until we finally arrived in mid-October at the Persian Gulf, where we planned to spend a few days engaged in ship-boarding exercises. It was October 12, a quiet Thursday morning right about lunchtime, when Jim McNary, our officer in charge (OIC), suddenly showed up in our berthing area with some unexpected and sobering news. One of our destroyers, the USS *Cole*, had been hit and was in danger of sinking.

Holy shit, we all thought.

Shortly after eleven o'clock that morning, a small powerboat just off the coast of nearby Yemen, loaded with a quarter ton of homemade explosives and manned by a total of two as-yet-unidentified assailants, had sidled up to the ship on its port side and detonated, blowing a forty-by-forty-foot hole in the *Cole*'s hull.

Two guys in a little speedboat did this?

Yes, two guys. Seventeen American sailors had died, thirty-nine others were wounded, and a gigantic U.S. warship was dangerously close to sinking. Immediate support was needed. Other naval personnel would labor to save the vessel from sinking, and still others would play an investigative role and work to nail down exactly who it was who did this thing. As SEALs, our job was to button the place down and provide impenetrable security.

Within eight hours we had made the clockwise loop through the Persian Gulf, the Gulf of Oman, the Arabian Sea, and the Gulf of Aden, and were in the Port of Yemen boarding the crippled hulk of the *Cole*.

An acrid smell from the explosion still hung in the air, but as we climbed aboard the *Cole* that odor was quickly overtaken by another, far worse smell. The carnage was awful, with rotting food and decomposing bodies under the hot Middle Eastern sun.

I'll never forget that smell.

Command had serious concerns that there might still be

unexploded ordnance, so some of our guys went to work searching the vessel while others circled out on the water and maintained a defensive perimeter around the harbor. Meanwhile Glen and I, fresh from our sniper school training, joined the platoon's two more experienced snipers up on the *Cole*'s bridge and began round-the-clock overwatch rotations with a full complement of weapons at the ready. Our orders were unambiguous: If anyone came within a hundred yards of that ship, we were cleared to use deadly force.

Our reaction when we heard those orders was raised eyebrows, followed by fist pumps. These were unusually aggressive ground rules. Ask any Spec Op warrior about ROEs (rules of engagement) and he will tell you they are seldom our friends. As SEALs we are trained to operate independently in any situation, which means we're expected to use our own judgment and make snap life-and-death, mission-critical decisions. In essence, every SEAL is a fully operational army of one. The last thing we want is to be second-guessed on the battlefield by shortsighted restrictions motivated by political considerations parsed from comfy armchairs thousands of miles from the realities of war. Unfortunately the typical ROEs in situations of armed conflict more often reflect the conditions on Capitol Hill than those on the battlefield. In years to come, such timid and impractical ROEs would routinely drive us nuts. But not here on the bridge of the *Cole*. Right now our orders were simple: "Anyone approaches without permission, shoot to kill."

As snipers it was our job to maintain constant, 100 percent, 360-degree situational awareness and threat assessment. What were the strengths and weaknesses of our position? Where were threats most likely to come from? At any given moment, what should we be most focused on—and what was happening everywhere else? Glen and I and the other two snipers spent hours at a stretch on the spotting scope or binos, surveilling every inch of the harbor, Win Mag at the ready, different sectors arranged in our heads and accurate ranges dialed in on our scopes so that if at any second we had to take a shot, we'd be prepared and not have to scramble to set our parameters.

Meanwhile the *Cole* was slowly sinking under our feet. Our team of naval engineers brought in special equipment to keep the bilges pumping and the ship afloat. If someone farted in the wrong direction, that boat was going down. It almost sank a few times right there in port.

As we watched the shore, the shore was watching us.

Yemen was not exactly the most U.S.-friendly nation in the Middle East. The Yemeni military forces had their weapons trained on us, which meant that the guys we were staring at through our binos were peering at us through *their* binos. It felt like a high-tech Mexican standoff. Technically speaking, they were our hosts; after all, we were tied up to their pier. But what did we really know about them? Were they in sympathy with the guys who'd just blown up our ship? Had they *sent* those guys? We had no way of knowing. It was eerie. And it went on like that for days, while our naval engineering crews furiously pumped out the putrid bilgewater and struggled to keep the ship from giving up the ghost and sloughing off to rest at the bottom of the Port of Aden.

Within twelve hours after we first arrived, a team of FBI agents was on the scene, soon followed by a Naval Criminal

Investigative Service detail and a crew from the CIA. This was some serious shit. Most of the world didn't yet fully grasp what had happened, and few would understand its implications until eleven months later, when the World Trade Center would lie in blood-soaked ruins.

We hadn't just been attacked by a few rogue terrorists. We had entered a new age of warfare.

In the Civil War, long lines of soldiers armed with bayonet-clad rifles massed into great walls of firepower, facing off in leaden hailstorms of Minié balls and black powder, just as Xerxes and the Spartans had faced off with spears and shields. In World War II, Patton's and Rommel's tank battalions pummeled one another in the African desert. In Desert Storm, fleets of warplanes wreaked such rapid and complete devastation on Saddam's offensive line that ground troops were practically an afterthought. As the tools of war evolved, the form of battle changed, but it was all fundamentally the same tactic: Line up the biggest mass of weaponry you can and hurl it at the enemy with all the force you've got.

But not with the *Cole*. Here the old rules of engagement no longer applied. A crappy little speedboat manned by two guys had just crippled and nearly sunk a billion-dollar, ten-thousand-ton warship, killed and wounded dozens of sailors, and inflicted some $250 million in damages on the mightiest military force on earth. This wasn't conventional warfare, and it wasn't even guerrilla warfare. This was *asymmetrical* warfare—a brand-new kind of war where mass meant nothing and intelligence meant everything.

And there was one guy on our team who understood this better than anyone else there: our assistant officer in charge, Dave Scott.

. . .

Dave was new to the platoon. In fact, he had joined us as third officer (number three in the platoon's officer command chain, what we call third O) just a few weeks before we deployed.

Dave was a substantial guy, just over six feet, broad-shouldered and solid, an imposing presence. Whereas Mike Bearden stood like a Greek god, Dave was built like a tank and walked like a gorilla king, legs bowed slightly inward, yet spine always erect. His soft green eyes and lady-killer grin gave him a boyish charm that perfectly disguised the dangerous wit sizzling just below the surface. He clicked immediately with our platoon's chemistry and added a whole new layer of color to this already extremely crazy bunch. We all loved him right off the bat.

One thing we especially liked about Dave was that he was not one to toe the party line. His was the voice at the back of the room you could always count on to interrupt the speaker at the front of the room with a single "Bullshit!" His normally silky voice could be penetrating and commanding when he wanted it to be. He could easily silence an entire roomful of people, yet I never saw him yell or lose control. His sense of humor was pervasive and ruthless. He would not let a single opportunity pass to bust anyone's balls; nothing was sacred, no joke too obscene, no stunt too outrageous.

Dave was with a few buddies in line at an ATM one day (this was back in the States, a year or so before we met him) when a security guard started loading money into the machine. Dave noticed that the guy had a pistol strapped on but no magazine loaded in the well. The next thing his friends knew, Dave was sidling up to the guy from behind, one hand cradling a bunch of drinking straws he'd cribbed from a nearby juice stand. Thirty seconds later Dave was back in line and laughing his ass off, the poor security guard oblivious to the fact that his gun was now loaded with soda straws. If the place got robbed by the Cookie Monster this guy would have been all set; otherwise, he was in deep shit.

Who would have the balls to sneak up behind a security guard and mess with his gun? Only Dave. As I said, no boundaries. Dave's friends had a saying about him: "There are the rules that apply to everyone else—and then there are the rules that apply to Dave."

He was just as happy skewering himself and the SEALs as much as anyone else. Sometimes when he walked into a room he would glare at you and say in a bad Schwarzenegger voice, "We are here to get you out." Among his many tattoos, he had a line drawing of the Shadow, the old pulp-fiction vigilante crime fighter, inked in the middle of his back. "That's my shadow," he would say whenever someone pointed it out. "He watches my back."

One of Dave's favorite T-shirts was one he had printed with a quote from Jack Handey, the guy who wrote the "Deep Thoughts" segments on *Saturday Night Live* during the nineties:

If you're in a war, instead of throwing a hand grenade at the enemy, throw one of those small pumpkins. Maybe it'll make everyone think how stupid war is— and while they're thinking, you can throw a real grenade at them.

Dave was a wild man, a sort of mad genius. Over time we would learn just how wild he really was. But one thing we could see right away was that he was over-the-top brilliant.

With rare exceptions, Hollywood typically casts Spec Ops guys—Rangers, Green Berets, SEALs, and the rest—as macho, swaggering strongmen who converse in grunted monosyllables and chauvinistic clichés. As usual, Hollywood's got it wrong. If I had to identify the one skill set shared most by the men who become part of the SEAL teams, it would not be athletic ability, physical strength, or pugnacious attitude; it would be sheer brainpower. Yes, it takes a certain amount of physical grit to get through BUD/S and the rest of the training involved in becoming a full-fledged SEAL. But far more than that, it takes the ability to maintain laser-sharp mental focus under any conditions and to think your way out of insanely tight spots.

So as far as smarts go, the Naval Special Warfare bar is already fairly high. But Dave wasn't just smart. He was scary smart. For example, his savvy with electronics: He could make any gadget work, no matter how complicated it was or whether he'd ever seen it before. He would bring radio scanners with him in his car at the Burger King drive-through line and insert extra food items into other people's orders just to mess with them. Once when we were doing a night exercise, Dave figured out a way to rig a night-vision camera onto his helmet to record what everyone was doing, so we could later review everything that happened and learn how to improve. He also had a remarkable memory. We could pick up pretty much any piece of equipment we had on board—radio, night vision, a weapons system, intelligence system equipment, *anything*—and hand it to Dave, and no matter what it was, he could quote whole paragraphs verbatim from the manual.

He was also brilliant academically. Just weeks before joining our platoon he had finished up a course of study at the Elliott School of International Affairs at George Washington University, where he had taken a graduate-level course on political violence and terrorism taught by the renowned international terrorism expert Dr. Jerrold Post. Post, who would later author the pioneering text *The Mind of the Terrorist*, had become widely known for his psychological profile of Saddam Hussein after the invasion of Kuwait. Dave was big into the kind of nonstate actors that were still largely off the radar in those pre-9/11 days. Although the Soviet Union had been dead and buried for a decade, most still tended to think about major threats to national security in terms of hostile national forces, whether Saddam's Iraq, Khamenei's Iran, or Kim Jong-Il's North Korea. Not Dave. He was convinced that a far graver danger lay in more fuzzily defined and less clearly centralized terrorist groups.

Dave was more than a little prescient. It was as if he lived with one foot in the future. For his term paper in Dr. Post's class he chose what seemed like a fairly obscure topic at the time: He wrote a psychological profile of a shadowy Saudi dissident whom few outside the intelligence community had heard of. We didn't know this at the time, but the man Dave had written about just a few months before joining our platoon would turn out to be the mastermind behind the USS *Cole* bombing whose horrifying aftermath we were now witnessing.

The guy's name: Osama bin Laden.

. . .

For Dave, the worst thing about the nightmare of the *Cole* attack was that the whole damn thing seemed so fucking unnecessary. According to Dave, if any of our guys in this region had been paying attention, it would never have happened in the first place. Earlier that year, a group of terrorists had attempted to sink a nearly identical U.S. warship, the USS *The Sullivans*, in the same area, by identical tactics. In fact, they even used the same goddamn craft. Yes, you read that right: Although the earlier attack was foiled, the bad guys salvaged and repurposed that same crappy little speedboat, complete with its same homemade explosive charge, for a repeat performance later that year. Yemen was an openly anti-American nation, and the *Cole* was clearly in a dangerous and vulnerable position. The setup was obvious. But nobody was watching the store.

Dave had a good point. The level of security on the *Cole* before the bombing was ludicrous. A few guys had been placed to stand guard on the ship's rail with unloaded M-14s.

I have to repeat that: *unloaded* M-14s, as in, no ammo in the guns.

We were all in disbelief at the lack of preparation—except Dave, who was just disgusted. He was not at all surprised that the attack had happened. He had felt for years that the Navy and the military in general—the *country* in general— were far too lax in their approach to security. Nobody was talking much about identity theft or cyberattacks back in 2000—but Dave was. He was always extremely careful about personal information. Before coming on our deployment he had given his girlfriend, Kat, a list of phone numbers so she could reach the other guys in the platoon in case of an emergency. Reasonable enough, right? Only for Dave, just writing down the numbers wouldn't do. The numbers were all in code, and he gave her a mathematical formula she'd have to apply to the list to derive the actual phone numbers. He wasn't paranoid. He was just ten steps ahead of everyone else.

Dave was sitting with a few friends at a restaurant one day, talking about his Pennsylvania hometown. He grabbed a napkin and started drawing them a diagram: Over on the right was Philadelphia, the Main Line running northwest, and his town way over to the west—and then he stopped for a moment, looked at his friends, then bent over the napkin again and added a big lake, another major highway, and some mountains. "These aren't really there, okay?" he explained. "I'm just adding them in to confuse the bad guys, in case this napkin falls into the wrong hands."

He was joking, of course . . . but then again, that was the way Dave thought. He had a Special Forces OPSEC (operations security) mind-set all the time, no matter where he was or what he was doing.

Dave was an excellent operator and had no patience for what he saw as stupidity or incompetence. Outside of work, he was a tolerant guy who was slow to judge others and seldom held a grudge. When it came to work it was a different story. If someone screwed up in something work-related, he took it personally. If you were not up to the task or the mission, as far as Dave was concerned you were gone; you didn't exist. Despite his sarcasm and perpetual irreverence, he loved what he did and took it very seriously, and there was a rock-solid sense of patriotism hidden quiet at his core. He believed in this country and was mightily pissed off at how shoddy the general state of security and preparedness had become.

A day or two after we arrived at the *Cole*, we got word that someone had decided to provide cell phones to all the servicemen from the ship so they could call home to their families in the States. Most of us thought that was a pretty decent gesture. Dave was incensed.

"Those idiots," he said. "With a thirty-nine-dollar scanner from Radio Shack I could listen to every one of those calls!" He didn't stay quiet about it, either. He went straight to command and told them, "That's a really nice gesture, guys—but do you realize none of those calls are secure?"

Later that day Dave was out patrolling the harbor when someone started motoring toward the *Cole* in a small speedboat. When ordered to stop, the unidentified pilot just mouthed off and kept coming. *Probably a journalist*, figured Dave—but he kept his weapon trained on the approaching figure. He called up to the bridge and said, "Hey, if this idiot breaks the hundred-meter line, I'm shooting him." No reply came from the bridge, and Dave kept his sights glued to the guy, who kept drawing closer. He was two hundred meters away, then a hundred and fifty, then one twenty-five . . . and then the boat finally slowed, banked, and veered away. Definitely the healthier choice.

"Trust me," said Dave later, "if that guy had breached the line, I would have put my first shot in the engine block—and if that didn't stop him, the next shot would have been in *him*." I didn't doubt him for a moment. Dave was a graduate of the same NSW sniper course as Glen and me. He wouldn't have missed—and he wouldn't have hesitated, either. Dave had a pragmatic, old-school-warrior's view of the world. He didn't believe for a moment that "right" would necessarily triumph over "might" simply because the good guys were the good guys. The only way you triumphed over the bad guys was by being better at what you did than they were. And when it came to the prospect of killing them, he wasn't the least bit squeamish.

It took a few weeks to make the *Cole* ready for transport back to the States. Finally they loaded it onto a gigantic transport ship, the Norwegian MV *Blue Marlin*, and as the vessel pulled away and out toward open sea, the crew started playing some macho Kid Rock song on a set of loudspeakers.

"*Bullshit*," Dave's voice cut through. "I can't believe you guys—that's the *wrong* song to be playing right now!"

As far as Dave was concerned, we'd just lost. The other guys got the better of us and there was nothing to be proud of here. We fucked up, and they won; it was that simple. I'm sure the crew saw it differently. Theirs was a huge and difficult task: They had to keep the damn thing afloat, put out all the fires, ready it for transport and salvage, and do all that and more under the creepily hostile gaze of foreign nationals who seemed all too ready to shoot at them. So, hey, credit where credit was due. But to Dave there was nothing there to celebrate.

"We are in deep shit," he mused as the *Blue Marlin* and its crippled freight pulled away. We sure were. Dave just saw it before the rest of us did.

Dave's radiant intelligence was just one facet of his outsize personality. The other was an unbridled wildness. These two sides of Dave contrasted so starkly that it was as if he were two different people, each one pulling his life in opposite directions—a brainy technology nerd who required extreme physical risk the way the rest of us need oxygen. Apollo and Dionysus, god of rational thinking and god of chaos and the outrageous, wrapped into a single person.

To a degree, I related to that crazy risk-taker side of Dave. From the moment I could crawl I was a daredevil, constantly getting myself into trouble, courting danger, and pushing things to extremes. I made my poor mother's life hell; she says it was a wonder I survived childhood, let alone adolescence. But Dave? He took recklessness to a whole new level. I could never be as extreme or outrageous as Dave, and wasn't even sure I'd want to be. But I admired the hell out of his raw courage and sheer mental appetite.

While still in grade school, Dave asked his parents if he could take computer lessons—and this was in the early eighties, when personal computers were not yet popular. (Dave was born in 1973, a month after Mike Bearden and a year before me.) He would sit for hours messing around with his Franklin, an early competitor of the Apple II. And it wasn't about playing games; he would sit there and program the damn thing. He personified "computer geek" before anyone had invented the term.

At the same time, he lived for physical thrills. Even from his earliest days, Dave was an adrenaline junkie. He loved being outside on his bike and using it to do the riskiest tricks possible. His dad helped him build a half-pipe in the backyard, where he practiced his bike moves for hours. They attached a zip line to Dave's tree fort so he could go shooting down it with a banshee cry, practicing his feats of aerial derring-do.

The Scotts had a vacation home on the nearby Jersey coast, and by age three Dave was addicted to plunging into the ocean, no matter the water temperature. He would thrash around in the freezing-cold surf, lips turning blue, teeth chattering, and if anyone suggested it was time to get out, he'd say, "I'm n-n-not c-c-c-cold!" The cold just didn't seem to bother him. One day his dad, Jack, found him playing around in a mudflat by the beach, rolling around down in the mud, doing push-ups. "He was so completely covered in mud," says Jack, "all you could see were his eyes."

The dude hadn't even started kindergarten yet and he was already putting himself through BUD/S.

A decade and a half later, on a simmering Friday evening in July of 1990, when Dave was about to enter his senior year of high school, a summer blockbuster came out. *Navy SEALs*, starring Charlie Sheen, did a few million at the box office that first weekend, no more than a modest splash for a summer action film. But it ignited a lot of young men's souls, including Dave's. He walked out of that suburban theater with the siren song of life as a SEAL pounding in his blood.

At the same time, the world of numbers and electrons held as powerful an attraction as ever. A National Merit scholar, Dave graduated high school with excellent SAT scores, then enrolled in Penn State to study computer engineering. It looked for a while like the academic brain might hold sway over the thrill-seeker gene. But Dave quickly grew bored with college and couldn't bring himself to sit through his classes. Soon he wasn't even showing up for them. He gave it a year before dropping out.

When he called his parents to break the news that he was joining the Navy, they were aghast. Maggie Scott, Dave's mother, burst into tears on the phone and did everything she could to persuade him to change his mind. As her husband, Jack, says, "I heard some words from her mouth I heard only then and during childbirth." Maggie sums it up this way: "We were not happy." But they both knew that nothing they could do would budge him.

In 1993, two years after finishing high school, Dave went through BUD/S Class 195. He then spent the next few years in deployments with his SEAL team in various parts of the world.

One Sunday morning during these years, the phone rang in the Scott home in the Philadelphia suburbs. When Maggie picked up she was surprised and delighted to hear Dave's voice on the other end. "Dave!" she exclaimed, beckoning to Jack to pick up an extension. "How are you?"

"Better than I was," said Dave. He was calling from a hospital bed in Quito, Ecuador. "I was in a little accident," he explained.

As his parents listened, horrified, he related the sketchiest details of his "little" accident. It had happened about a week earlier, in the middle of the night, and it involved a car crash somewhere along the Ecuador-Colombia border. That was all they ever knew. The story we heard on the teams was that he and some buddies had gotten into it with some locals and were speeding away from the banditos when their car rolled. One Golf Platoon teammate says he heard Dave was on a motorcycle at the time. Whatever actually happened, Dave had been badly hurt, his colon perforated and his insides pretty much torn out.

Dave was taken to a clinic in the area, but when they saw a sonogram the clinicians on staff knew they were way out of their depth. Dave was medevaced out to emergency surgery in Quito, where he lay wide-open on an operating table for an extended series of procedures, including the removal of a few inches of intestine that were not salvageable. (We could see the evidence whenever Dave took off his shirt: a huge, ugly scar ran some ten inches vertically from his lower gut up to his rib cage. "Hey, check it out," he'd say. "You wanna see some cut abs?")

After being shuttled through several different hospitals, Dave eventually arrived back at Walter Reed in Bethesda. Jack and Maggie fetched him out of the hospital and brought him back home for some brief recuperation time before he could go in and have his colon reattached. Meanwhile, Dave had to wear a colostomy bag—which he lost no time using to good advantage when he was back at NSW headquarters in Virginia Beach for a short stretch before his reattachment surgery.

Every SEAL team has a floor in the Naval Special Warfare building where all the paperwork, travel claims, and other administration happens. This is where the CO's office is located, and it's also where nobody in the platoon wants to be. (We'd all rather be hanging out in our platoon's team room.)

Dave would let his colostomy bag fill up with gas, then sneak upstairs into the main hallway in his PT gear, open the valve, and squeeze its contents out into the open air. He delighted in describing the results to us in graphic detail. "Man, that stench was so nasty and teargas powerful, people would *run* for the exit with their eyes watering. It would clear the building." And he took such unadulterated pleasure in it that he'd do it all over again the next day. I'll never forget Dave's evil grin as he painted the scene for us. He called it "Saddam gassing the Kurds." Totally tasteless, I know. We all laughed so hard we thought we might end up with internal injuries and colostomy bags, too.

Following Dave's exploits in South America, the pendulum swung the other way for a while, as the incandescently brilliant side of his personality decided it was hungry. Leaving the teams, he enrolled at the Elliott School in D.C. to pursue his bachelor's in international affairs with a concentration in counterterrorism and national security—the same program where he would soon take that course with Dr. Post and write his paper on bin Laden. For the next few years he funneled his explosive kinetic energy into academics, completing the four-year program within two years. "You know," he told his parents, "it's really not that hard if you actually study and go to class."

But he desperately wanted to get back into the field. Without telling Jack or Maggie, he enrolled in ROTC at the same time so he would walk out of George Washington with his officer's commission as well as a bachelor's degree. (Dave was what we call a "mustang"—that is, an officer who started out as an enlisted man. The term comes from the idea that a mustang horse can be tamed and saddle-broken but always maintains its wild streak—a definition tailor-made for Dave.) It wasn't until he was halfway through his program that he confessed to his parents about the ROTC track and his intention to return to the teams. When they grilled him as to why on earth he would give up a brilliant and promising academic career to return to the SEALs, he said, "I still can't believe I actually get paid to jump out of airplanes, shoot guns, and blow things up!"

SEAL officer billets are highly competitive. The U.S. Naval Academy gives out the majority of them and allows only sixteen spots per year. Half that number go to ROTC programs and are competed for across all the top colleges in the nation. The odds of getting a SEAL officer billet were extremely low—but as a formerly deployed SEAL, Dave was already in the club, and his work at the Elliott School had also made him well connected. On top of all that he was extremely well liked by his peers. If it took bending a rule in Dave's favor to allow him back into the teams as an officer, the chances were good that would happen. Sure enough, immediately after graduating he was in Coronado reporting to Team Three, the ink barely dry on his re-up papers, and wangling his way onto our platoon, where we instantly accepted him into our tight-knit group. Two weeks later he was with the rest of us on the USS *Duluth*, bound for the Middle East and our rendezvous with the crippled USS *Cole*.

Once the *Cole* was loaded onto a freighter and hauled away and we were released from the Port of Aden, we returned to Bahrain, where we finally did get in some ship-boarding exercises. But we weren't there long.

After the *Cole* was hit, nobody had any idea what attacks might be coming next, so the Navy immediately halted all resupply operations that were under way throughout the region and rerouted everything through a single port, where they could focus all their surveillance and intelligence resources in one place to make sure it was all safe. The guys in charge of making sure it was safe were us.

While nobody came out and said so, it was clear that command was worried about another *Cole*-style attack on an

American vessel. If two idiots in a crappy little powerboat could take out a ten-thousand-ton destroyer, then who knew what else was possible? The security of the entire overseas fleet depended on our ability to get these resupply ships in and out safely.

Since there was a substantial population of expat British and American workers in this particular port, it was relatively easy for us to blend in. We took twelve-hour shifts, setting up surveillance in the port either early in the morning or at night, depending on our rotation. Just like on the bridge of the *Cole*, we spent long hours doing nothing but watching through our optics and binos, watching anything and everything. Why was that truck over there? Trucks weren't supposed to be there. Who were these guys over here who weren't here yesterday, and what were they doing here today? Anything remotely suspicious we wrote down in our activity logs, which would later be turned into reports that would go up some unseen chain of intelligence command.

We were not authorized to have weapons outside a certain zone in the port—but authorized or not, we carried concealed sidearms anyway, not just when in our hotel but everywhere around town, which added another layer of tension to the situation.

In this exotic locale we had a firsthand experience of the incredibly byzantine puzzle that is Middle Eastern culture and politics. There was the constant sense that we were missing huge chunks of the full picture. American forces have gotten somewhat better at this in the years since 9/11, but back then we were relatively unprepared. We knew we were supposed to be functioning in essence as a crew of intelligence operatives, but it was hard not to feel like a bunch of ridiculously conspicuous Caucasian Americans dropped in the middle of what might as well have been a distant planet. There were so many cultures, dialects, religious sects, dynastic families . . . it was an immense tangle of nuance and history, shifting alliances and ancient grudges. We felt enveloped by a sense of helplessness: How the hell could we possibly understand what was going on here?

And, of course, Dave absolutely loved it. For him it was like Christmas morning. Complexity? Cultural ambiguity? Undercurrents of espionage and international intrigue? Risk of discovery and grave danger to one's person? *Yes!* The dude was in his element. The only thing missing was high-altitude, high-octane physical danger—and, of course, the opportunity to actually kill bad guys.

With his hair worn long and an earring in one ear, Dave gave the perfect impression of being an eccentric computer geek. (Which, of course, he *was*.) He would work at the computers for hours, then go to work up on the roof with sniper scopes for hours more.

We spent a month gathering whatever information we could and passing it on up the channels. We also learned more about the Russian Mafia, the Middle Eastern sex-slave trade, and a whole raft of other immoral and illegal activities going on under our noses than we would have thought possible.

After completing the mission, we began our homeward trek across the Pacific. In February, on our way to Hawaii, we weighed anchor near the tiny island of Iwo Jima to participate in the fifty-sixth anniversary of the American Marine landing there during World War II.

This was, remember, a *Marine* landing we were commemorating, and the *Duluth* was full of Marines. The idea was that they would be the ones who would go ashore first. But Dave wasn't having any of that. Rather than wait around while the Marines boarded their boats and headed in, he jumped ship and swam ashore himself so he could reconnoiter ahead of everyone else. Once on land, he crafted a sign and posted it right at the beach's edge, facing outward so it would greet the Marines when they arrived:

U.S. MARINES
WELCOME TO IWO JIMA!
COURTESY OF SEAL TEAM 3

Dave had brought a container with him, which he proceeded to fill with forty pounds of pure black sand. After smuggling the sand back with him onto the *Duluth*, he measured it out into dozens of little bottles, then gave one to each Marine on board as a memento of his visit. A little bit of Iwo Jima to take home with them—courtesy of SEAL Team Three, of course.

This wasn't the last time our platoon would visit this part of the world. Dave and the other guys would be out this way again about a year and a half later, though I would not be with them that time—and that second trip would not end well.

Soon after we got back to the States, Dave became intensely interested in BASE jumping, which was just starting to gain popularity.

Coined in the 1970s, the term "BASE jumping" refers to

the act of jumping off a stationary object—BASE is an acronym for *b*uildings, *a*ntennae, *s*pans (bridges), and *e*arth (cliffs)—and using a parachute to land safely. Or attempting to. With a fatality rate more than forty times that of parachuting out of a plane, BASE jumping is the most dangerous recreational activity in the world.

Naturally Dave thought this was a fantastic idea. Kat, now his fiancée, was not so wild about it.

"The motorcycle thing I can live with," she told him. "The skydiving I'm not totally crazy about, but it's something you have to do for work anyway, and you seem to know what you're doing. But BASE jumping? Sorry—that's where I draw the line."

Dave and Kat had met at George Washington, just as she was about to begin her sophomore year. (Like Dave, she was there on an ROTC program and bound for active duty in the Navy.) Everyone on campus knew that this guy had just come off two tours as a Navy SEAL, and he was the talk of the campus. "All the girls' tongues were wagging," says Kat, "and all the guys wanted to be his best friend. My eyes rolled as far back in my head as they could and I thought, 'You've *got* to be kidding me.' I wanted nothing to do with him. I just knew he was trouble."

Much to Kat's dismay, when the fall semester began she found she'd been assigned as part of an ROTC sophomore-to-freshman buddy system to tour the new SEAL guy around the campus and show him the ropes. Dave soon discovered that Kat was not only gorgeous, she was also brilliant—and she had no trouble keeping up with his laser wit. The two quickly became fast friends. By the following year they were dating.

"Kat is the first girlfriend I've ever had who's smarter than I am," Dave told us when he joined our platoon a year later. Still, being in a relationship with Dave was anything but easy, even for someone as resourceful as Kat. When it came to BASE jumping she had put her foot down, but she knew better than anyone that Dave was impossible to contain.

In mid-2001, while Kat was in Newport, Rhode Island, going through her six months of surface warfare training before reporting to her fleet, Dave told her he had to go out of town for a couple of days and might not be able to call while he was gone. A few days later he called and said, "I have something to tell you, and I think you're going to be mad at me."

Kat's heart leaped into her throat. Dave was incredibly charming, and she had no illusions that the long periods apart were easy on either of them. Had he met someone else? Was their relationship in trouble?

There was a silence on the phone. Then Dave said, "I took a BASE jumping course."

Even in the midst of her relief, Kat knew damn well she had just been played.

That summer I transferred to a different platoon within SEAL Team Three, one that was scheduled for deployment to the Middle East later that year. I loved Golf Platoon, the group I'd been with, and absolutely hated the idea of leaving Glen Doherty, Mike Ritland, Shane Hiatt, Dave Scott, and all my other close buddies behind. But ops at command had asked if I would join Echo, a weaker platoon, to help it get on its feet. I was by now newly married and we were expecting our first child. They were offering me a substantial bonus to make the lateral move to boost this fucked-up platoon—an offer I couldn't refuse. I said a reluctant good-bye to Glen and Dave and the rest of my teammates at Golf Platoon and joined Echo.

It turned out to be a more fateful decision than I could have imagined: The events of September 11 were only weeks away.

In the wake of the 9/11 attacks, my new platoon was one of the first to put boots on the ground in Afghanistan. Our task: to rout out and destroy every Taliban or al Qaeda element we could find. That December, while Dave and Kat were being married in a ceremony at the chapel at Walter Reed (they had actually eloped in June, but held the December ceremony for friends and family), I was threading my way in the pitch-black through a warren of mountain caves in northern Afghanistan, jammed up against the Pakistan border. On that mission, along with huge caches of weapons and matériel, we discovered al Qaeda recruiting posters with Photoshopped pictures of airplanes crashing into the World Trade Center towers—posters that had been made up and circulated within this network in the months *before* the attacks. It was beyond creepy. We found nearly a million pounds of ammunition, equipment, and intelligence resources—and we dropped close to half a million pounds of ordnance, taking out one of the largest terrorist training facilities in the country.

Meanwhile Dave was back stateside with the other guys, frustrated beyond description that the biggest conflict in years was happening on the other side of the world, and he wasn't there in the middle of it. It only added further fuel to the fire of Dave's constant hunger for physical adventure.

The following spring, while she was shipboard on an exercise, Kat got an e-mail from Dave. Something was wrong, but he wouldn't say what it was in the e-mail. He just left her a phone number. When she called the number she found she was talking to a hospital in Memphis. Dave had been in an accident. "We were skydiving," he told her. "I had a bad landing and got a little banged up, but no big deal. I'm flying home tomorrow."

When she returned to port in San Diego the following day and picked Dave up from the airport, she was shocked to see the condition he was in. Clearly he was not just "a little banged up." His face was a mess and he was using a walker. He looked bad.

Kat didn't learn this till a few years later, but in fact Dave had not been skydiving. He'd been BASE jumping.

While training at the famous Shaw Shooting range in Mississippi, Dave and another Team Three guy took off to do a BASE jump off a balcony near the top of a very tall Memphis hotel. Somehow Dave opened facing toward the building, swung back and slammed into it, then scraped his way all the way down the side of the building until he collided with a massive concrete planter. In addition to messing up his face and chipping some teeth, Dave had a hairline fracture in his pelvis—and a lacerated liver. A lacerated liver is no laughing matter. If he hadn't gotten immediate medical attention he could easily have bled out and died.

Although his injuries were severe, Dave recuperated at home and went back to work much sooner than anyone wanted him to. He said he was bored sitting around the apartment. Kat was about to go on deployment herself and knew she wouldn't be able to get much time off to help him hobble around.

Dave didn't mind being bashed up. He just shrugged and took it in stride. To him, getting injured was part of the risk. But he had absolutely no patience with the recuperation process and couldn't stand being laid up and stationary. Like a shark, Dave had to be in motion or he felt like he was dying.

Dave also craved intellectual simulation every bit as much as physical adventure. While he recouped from his Mississippi BASE jump, if he couldn't use his body, at least he could engage his mind. He took up Tagalog (pronounced *ti-GAH-lug*), the native language of the Philippines. He knew the platoon would be returning to that part of the world soon, and he figured the ability to speak the native language would be an advantage there.

In fact, any leg up he could gain in the area of intelligence was a big plus at this point. Dave was already planning to leave the service and get into contract security work after his next deployment. He'd interviewed with the CIA, and he knew damn well that with his intelligence background and uncanny grasp of the shadowy world of al Qaeda–style international networks, he was any intelligence analyst's wet dream. When his parents asked him what he planned to do next, he told them the CIA had declined to hire him, and he would be doing some other kind of work instead. But that was just classic Dave smoke-screen bullshit. He would do anything and say anything to protect his parents and keep them from worrying. He was CIA-bound for sure. Dave knew that cyberterrorism and advanced intelligence were where the action of the future lay, and wherever the frontier of war was, that was where he wanted to be.

In July 2002, Kat set off on a guided missile cruiser, USS *Mobile Bay*, for a deployment in the Persian Gulf, where as deck division officer she would be standing bridge watch and leading boarding parties on missions very similar to some I'd participated in on my way to Afghanistan, right after 9/11.

Dave was there that July to see her off. On the bridge of the huge vessel there hung a large hand-drawn banner that read, WE SHALL NEVER FORGET.

By this time I was back from Afghanistan. Iraq was heating up, with war clearly on the horizon. It looked like my old platoon would be rotating into the action, if Iraq did indeed blow up. Meanwhile, they were about to head westward again. Two months later Golf Platoon—which still included Glen, Mike Ritland, Shane, and all my other close friends from our USS *Cole* days—deployed once again across the South Pacific, headed toward the Philippines. Dave had been moved over to Delta Platoon with a billet as assistant officer in charge (AOIC), or second O, but Delta was Golf's sister platoon, and the two groups deployed together.

On the way west they stopped over for a while in the U.S. territory of Guam. While it is a strategically important stepping-stone to Asia, it's hard to describe adequately just how remote Guam is. With a total area about the size of Columbus, Ohio (that's about one-twentieth the area of the island of Hawaii), Guam is a minuscule dot in the middle of the vast Pacific. When you're stationed on Guam, you might as well be on the moon. Dave was antsy.

One day while doing a little sightseeing, Mike Ritland,

Shane, and Dave were standing at a famous cliffside spot on Guam's northwestern coast, just above Tumon Bay. Called Two Lovers Point, the place features a traditional statue depicting the two lovers from an ancient native Romeo-and-Juliet-type legend. Forbidden to marry, the two leaped from this cliff together to be wedded forever in death. It's a dramatic spot. You stand on a cantilevered balcony and look straight down through a four-hundred-foot drop to the waves and rocks below.

As Mike and Shane gazed out at the ocean's westward expanse, they heard a *pock, pock, pock* down below. Dave was chucking pebbles off the edge and timing how long it took them to hit water with his Casio G-Shock wristwatch. "That crazy bastard," says Mike. "He was checking the place out for a goddamn BASE jump!"

After a few weeks in Guam, Golf Platoon moved on westward to the Philippines to put in some time helping the Filipino SEALs in their fight against the Abu Sayyaf Group (ASG), a long-standing militant Islamist organization. The ASG were high on our list of bad guys in the still-young War on Terror, and going up against them was a top priority. Our role was to train. While our guys trained one group of Filipino SEALs to help them improve their tactics, a second group would head south to Zamboanga to go head-to-head with ASG forces, then come back up north and rotate out with the first group.

Meanwhile Delta, Dave's platoon, stayed behind in Guam, where Dave was stuck doing boring tasks for his CO—while barely fifteen hundred miles away his buddies were engaged (albeit indirectly) in fighting terrorists. So much for mastering Tagalog. It must have driven Dave stir-crazy.

One quiet Saturday in October, Mike Ritland, Shane, Glen, and the others were all called into their OIC's hotel room in the Philippines. "Hey," the OIC said, his face a blank. "I've got something I need to tell you guys."

Back in Guam, Dave had gone BASE jumping—not off Two Lovers Point, but at Orote Point, a remote location out on the westernmost tip of the island, not far from the naval base there. Just like the balcony at Two Lovers, it was a four-hundred-foot drop from a lush green cliff straight down to the ocean's surface.

Based on the evidence, and knowing how Dave operated, it was not hard to reconstruct what had happened. He would have made a thorough study of the elevation, the tide and currents, the wind, and every factor affecting the jump. Once fully prepared, he hurled himself off the cliff and into the open air. The jump was perfect. Pulling himself out of the surf, he gathered his chute and started back up the path leading up the face of the cliff. And then something ridiculous happened. Something so out of character that if Dave had been standing nearby watching himself, he would have had a field day busting his own balls: He slipped and fell from the path. The fall fractured his skull; by the time they found him, he was gone.

It was October 12, two years to the day since the bombing of the USS *Cole*.

Back in the Philippines, Mike, Shane, and Glen filed out of their OIC's room in shock, no one saying a word. They were all thinking the same thing. *No fucking way. Not Dave. Not possible. This did* not *happen.* One by one they all made their way back to their rooms. A few minutes later they rejoined and went outside for a run. Mike still remembers that run: nothing but the sounds of hard breathing and feet slapping the ground to underscore the deepening silence, each man alone in his own thoughts.

Later the three went out to a place they knew and had a few drinks together. Sitting around the table in that little Filipino bar, no one said a word, the silence stretching out beneath the dull hum of a slow ceiling fan. Then Glen gripped his shot glass of tequila and hoisted it into the air.

"To Dave," he said. Nobody else moved. Glen looked at Shane, then at Mike.

"Look," he said, "I know we're all hurting. But we all signed up for this. Dave wasn't on the job, technically speaking—but it's all the same thing. It's part of the fucking deal. So let's not sit here feeling sorry for him. He wouldn't want that. And none of us would want that, either, if we were in his shoes. Dave was a hell of a guy. Let's drink up and celebrate his life."

Glen's impromptu speech began pulling the other two out of their funk. They all drank to Dave and started recounting his exploits, which were legion.

Although I wasn't there with them at the time, I heard about the scene later from Mike Ritland, and Glen's words struck deep. They would come back to me, and strike even deeper, exactly ten years later.

Kat flew home to be present when they buried Dave at Arlington with military honors, two weeks after his death. Bob Harward, our CO, gave a tribute to Dave, and spoke the traditional words that all veterans know: "Mrs. Scott, on behalf of the president of the United States, a grateful nation, and a proud Navy, this flag is presented as a token of our appreciation for the honorable and faithful service rendered by your loved one to his country and the Navy."

Mike, Shane, and Glen wanted badly to fly back to the States to be there for the funeral, and Kat lobbied for permission for them to come, but it didn't happen. Mike and his wife were close friends with Dave and Kat, and for years afterward Mike felt shitty that he couldn't be there for Kat. He would eventually get a sense of closure with Dave's passing, but not for many years.

The Navy offered Kat a desk to ride, but she knew that would be depressing and miserable. She opted instead to get back on her ship. When the Shock and Awe campaign began the following April, Kat was on her cruiser in the Gulf, launching guided missiles into Baghdad and watching them explode in real time on CNN.

Back in 1999, when Dave was at the Elliott School in D.C., he had a good friend, an ex–Navy corpsman who was now with the Marine Force Reconnaissance, named Greg Skelton. One day Greg challenged Dave to compete in the Marine Corps Marathon, a footrace of more than twenty-six miles. Dave took the challenge and, Dave being Dave, he also immediately upped the ante and insisted they run it "the Navy SEAL way," in "boots and utes," in other words, wearing a T-shirt and camouflage pants (utility uniform) and combat boots.

Greg called his bluff. "Let's do it," he said.

So they did. It wasn't until eighteen miles into the race that Dave glanced over at Greg as they ran and said, "Hey . . .

I don't know if . . . you realize this, but . . . I was just kidding about . . . the boots and utes." They huffed another twenty yards or so; then Dave added, "But what the hell, we've . . . come this far; let's . . . finish this fucker." And they did—the only runners among the thirty thousand participants who ran the competition, let alone finished it, in heavy boots.

In October 2003, exactly one year after Dave's death, Greg ran the Marine Corps Marathon again, once again with a Scott by his side—Dave's dad, Jack, standing in for his absent son. When they reached the finish line Jack didn't stop running. After another half mile he finally slowed and came to a standstill at Arlington National Cemetery, where he draped his finisher's medal over Dave's grave site.

The following year Greg couldn't make it, but Dave's younger brother, Mike, kept the tradition going and ran the race himself. Like his father the year before, Mike continued on to Arlington to leave his Marine Corps Marathon finisher's medal on his brother's grave.

The year after that, Greg was determined not to miss the event: He drove in uniform nonstop from Georgia to D.C. to run the race one more time—in boots and utes. Leaving the finish line behind, he followed in Jack's and Mike's footsteps until he had reached Dave's final resting place, where he added a third medal to his friend's growing collection.

Dave was the embodiment of the expression *larger than life*. Everything he did, he took to a level beyond what anyone else would think possible. He was more hilarious, more outrageous, more audacious. As his mom, Maggie, put it, "Dave lived more in his twenty-nine and a half years than others could live in a hundred."

Because he was so quick, he could pick up on anything that anyone was talking about and find a way to reference it to something he knew about or had experience with. That high-speed intelligence, combined with his basic good nature and sense of humor, gave him an amazing gift for conversation and for striking up new friendships. Kat describes him as a chameleon: He could throw wild parties filled with sophomoric stunts (like the time he convinced a group of starstruck freshmen to prove their mettle by sweating it out in a bathroom with an ignited teargas grenade Dave just happened to have hung on to from an earlier SEAL deployment), and the next day walk into any posh D.C. eating or drinking establishment and chat up the worldly professionals you'd find there as if he were one of them. Dave could talk to anybody and make anyone laugh.

In many ways Dave was like a big kid. There was absolutely no situation where he would not let loose with his crazy grin, booming laugh, and insane antics, if he was so moved. His Elliott School roommate DeVere Crooks remembers being in the shower at the end of a long day of study, when suddenly a giant gorilla arm shot in from around the shower curtain and turned off the hot water. DeVere almost had a Janet Leigh–style heart attack. Classic Dave.

"He had the most tender of hearts, a boyish imagination, and a bold vision of where he wanted to be," says Kat. "I often wonder if I mistakenly caught a bolt of lightning. After so many years, it still saddens me to think of that light as not being there anymore."

For me Dave's life stands both as an inspiration and as a cautionary tale. I've always been drawn to extreme sports. There's nothing I love quite so much (my early qualms notwithstanding) as throwing myself out of a perfectly good airplane. All my life I've taken things to the edge. All SEALs do; it's our job description. But Dave took things right to the edge and then well past it. In a way, it was amazing that he lived as long as he did. That insatiable appetite for what lay beyond the edge is no doubt what killed him. Yet it was also what made him so brilliant. Dave understood the twenty-first century when most of us still thought we were living in the twentieth. And his intelligence was infectious. Just being around him made me more curious about how things worked—and even more important, how they *could* work.

About a year after Dave died, my friend and BUD/S classmate Eric Davis and I were recruited to take on the complete revamping and redesign of the Naval Special Warfare sniper course. It was an enormous task and an even greater responsibility (and one we'll look at more in the next chapter). The world had changed dramatically since the bombing of the *Cole*, and so had the nature of warfare—and even more, the role that SEAL snipers played. We needed a new course, one that left behind the past and addressed the future. We needed a course that incorporated the latest in technological wizardry, that fully developed its trainees intellectually as well as physically, a course that would be designed for continuous improvement so that it would always be ten steps ahead. A course that pushed the envelope to the edge of the possible, and then pushed it even further.

We needed a course, in other words, that thought like Dave Scott.

I can never hope to be as smart as Dave. But in the years

since I knew him I've made it a practice to examine the world around me through his eyes. The Dionysus in Dave still taunts me today, daring me to look past my limits—and the Apollo in Dave is always there to help me grasp what I see there.

3

QUIET PROFESSIONAL

MATT AXELSON

"Listen up, gents. The next ninety days are going to be some of the toughest you've ever experienced. You'll be put under more pressure and greater mental demands than you've ever been under before, and with zero tolerance given for error. . . ."

Déjà vu. I'd heard this speech before, or one much like it. Back in the summer of 2000, Glen and I had been inducted into the Naval Special Warfare sniper course with a welcoming pep talk just like this one. The world had gone through a century of change in the four years since. It was now the summer of 2004, and this time the guy giving that speech to a fresh batch of incoming sniper students was me.

"You'll be expected to deliver at a level of perfection that will at first seem unrealistic, unfair, and unreasonable. We will push the limits of your performance to such high levels that even when you are rusty, tired, or unpracticed you will still outperform the enemy. . . ."

As I spoke, the good citizens of San Diego were going about their lives several dozen feet above our heads, heedless of our subterranean presence.

I loved this underground setting and everything it represented. For our sniper class headquarters we had recently converted a set of old World War II–style bunkers built into the landscape on the south strand of Coronado. Put your back to the Pacific and you faced a monster set of doors, big enough to drive a truck through. Enter and walk through a breezeway, pass through another set of industrial double doors, and you were in our Naval Special Warfare complex, buried underneath south San Diego. You could keep walking and travel a good quarter mile under there. We had our own classrooms and offices, even our own armory where we stored all our cameras, guns, ammunition, and other gear behind a huge combination-lock safe door inches thick, like the door to a bank vault.

Standing in that bunker always made me think about being tunneled deep in the Hindu Kush mountains, threading our way through the Zhawar Kili cave complex in Afghanistan a few months after 9/11. I always savored the irony of being in this underground warren right off the southern California beaches. This was *our* cave complex, where we trained the guys who cleaned out those other cave complexes on the other side of the world.

When Dave Scott died in the fall of 2002, I was already back from my tour in Afghanistan and part of a training detachment, teaching a range of specialized classes as a sort of continuing-education program for our snipers. The following summer my friend and BUD/S classmate Eric Davis and I were tasked with the responsibility of helping completely revamp and transform the entire SEAL sniper course. The day we were called into our master chief's office and handed our new assignment still ranks as one of the greatest moments of my life. In effect, Naval Special Warfare command was putting an entire generation of snipers in our hands.

"You will come to know perfection as your new normal. And you'll be expected to deliver at that level of perfection day after grinding day without misstep, hiccup, or fuckup. . . ."

A lot had changed since Glen and I went through the course with Mike Bearden in the pre-9/11 days. We saw the shift foreshadowed in the bombing of the USS *Cole*, when an "insignificant" little two-man boat had taken out a billion-dollar warship. Eleven months later the scope and force of that shift were carved into concrete when two hijacked planes were shot, like steel-jacketed rifle shells from colossal rifles, into World Trade towers one and two. A full decade after the crash of the Soviet Union, we finally realized we were no longer living in an era when nations battled head-on like gladiators, and had stepped into the age of asymmetrical warfare.

The nature of modern war changed during those first few years of the new century, and with it the role of Special Operations. In the past Spec Ops was a relatively fringe element in our arsenal, called upon for unusual assignments here and there but used mainly to support the missions carried out by our conventional forces. There was a reason for the "special" in Special Operations.

But that distinction had now been turned on its head. Now we weren't going up against armies; we were pitted against shadowy leaders like Osama bin Laden and Ayman al-Zawahiri, and forces that faded into the scenery like morning mist and flowed over national boundaries like water. War itself had in effect morphed into Spec Ops warfare, and our Special Operations warriors—Navy SEALs, Army Rangers, Green Berets, Marine Force Recon, Air Force Combat Controllers/Pararescue Jumpers, and others—had gone from life as bastard stepchildren of the DOD to being the pointy tip of the spear. Which meant the demands on SEAL snipers had intensified dramatically.

Our job was to make sure the NSW sniper training stood up to the challenge and reflected the new world in which we now lived and fought.

"The men who graduated the classes before you are over in Iraq and Afghanistan right now, doing phenomenal work for the teams. They're cutting swaths through hotbeds of insurgency, carving out safe zones for our Marine and Army brothers to get in and operate without being picked off by enemy snipers or IEDs. They are the most effective snipers the global battlefield has ever seen. . . ."

Eric and I and our handpicked instructor cadre dived into our assignment like the combat divers we were, taking the course apart and completely reworking it, bottom to top. We brought in a huge range of advances and innovations, and trained our students in how to operate in situations where they had to deploy independently, rather than in traditional shooter/spotter pairs. We also put our instructors through more rigorous training so that they were all not only excellent technicians but also consistently good teachers; and much more. It was an ambitious and sweeping overhaul, and we had a blast sinking our teeth into it.

Over the first year of this assignment Eric and I had gone through four full iterations of our transformed course—and we were getting results. We were graduating better students and graduating more of them. In the old course, a failure rate of 30 percent or more was common. (In the summer of 2000, Glen's and my class flushed fourteen out of twenty-six starters, a loss of more than 50 percent.) Through the changes Eric and I implemented from summer 2003 through summer 2004, we had slashed that attrition down to less than 3 percent. By the time of my subterranean induction talk in June of 2004, we were graduating the highest percentage of students in the school's history, and producing the most highly skilled snipers the American armed forces had ever seen.

"This course will push you harder than you've ever been pushed, for a higher level of excellence than you've ever achieved. Halfway through you'll probably hate being here and wish you'd never signed up. . . ."

This was nothing like the first day of boot camp. No sullen expressions, no shuffling feet, no teenage anxieties trying their best to stay hidden under a mask of macho bluster. The two dozen men who stood before us were already highly trained professionals. These guys had survived BUD/S and gone through years of advanced SEAL training. Most had by this time been through at least one overseas deployment. Still, they were about to enter a three-month pressure cooker, and how they each responded would tell us volumes. I was watching them more closely than they probably realized.

Among the two dozen young men there, a few stood out immediately. It's always that way. As instructors, we'd trained ourselves not to trust our first impressions 100 percent—but damn close. In the field sometimes your gut feeling is your only compass, and if you can't act on it accurately and with precision, you might be dead before you get a second chance.

So even as I continued wrapping up my opening remarks, I was letting those first impressions sink in.

One guy in particular flagged my attention, a larger-than-life Texan. Later, when I had the chance to hear the students converse, I noticed that every time this one opened his mouth, what came out sounded like a cross between a country-western song and a gunslinger from the Old West getting ready to draw down. *This guy's trouble*, I thought with a smile. I meant that in a good way.

The kid standing next to him was obviously a close friend. You could see it from the way they glanced at each other now and then, sharing wordless snapshot reactions to something I'd said. The kid was slender and tall, well over six feet, short curly blond hair, thoughtful widely spaced eyes. In their brief round of introductions before my remarks began I'd learned he was from California but didn't quite catch his name. Quiet guy.

"But I can promise you this: If you give us every ounce of your attention, every calorie of energy, every percentage point of your focus and commitment, the instructors and I will do everything in our power to make sure you do make it through."

By the time my short talk was over I knew one thing: I would be assigning myself the loud Texan and his quiet friend as my personal students in our instructor-student mentor program. I wanted to keep my eyes on those two.

My gut told me they were quality.

The transformation of the SEAL sniper course was not just about techniques and technology. It was also a shift in how we related to our students and brought out the best they had to offer. Among the many changes we made in the course, one of the most significant had to do with the power of mentoring. Starting in 2004, we made it a regular practice to assign a specific instructor to each pair of students as their personal mentor. At a ratio of about six instructors to about twenty-four students per class, that meant every instructor typically had just two pairs of students to focus on personally.

Nothing trains a skill like the apprenticeship model, and this new system meant every student was essentially apprenticed to his own master. For us instructors, it also added a new competitive dimension to the course. Suddenly we each had a significant added motivation to make sure our students excelled: We wanted them to succeed not only for their sakes, but also because we wanted to kick *one another's* asses. SEAL instructors are every bit as competitive as their students.

Beyond all that, the mentoring program made the course personal. When you are assigned to teach a class of two dozen, that's one thing. But when you are responsible to individual students as their personal mentor, you cannot help getting emotionally invested in these men. Their success becomes your success, and their frustrations and challenges, whether or not they ever fully realize this fact, become your frustrations and challenges.

One of the first pairs of students I assigned myself to mentor was the tall Texan, whose name was Morgan Luttrell, and his friend, the kid from California, who despite his youthful energy was not a "kid" at all but twenty-seven years old, just a year younger than Luttrell (and for that matter just two years younger than me).

The quiet one's name was Matthew Axelson, but everyone called him Axe, which I thought was ironic, because if there was anyone who did *not* behave like an ax, it was this dude. Luttrell, now, he could swing a string of words over his head and probably split a cord of hardwood with them. Most of the men in the course could. This is not a demographic group known for their shyness or reticence. But Matt was the last person who would think of cutting anyone down, not even in fun.

As the course got under way, it also became obvious that the other guys looked up to Matt. This surprised me at first, because he was so quiet. Typically the ones the others look up to—guys like Mike Bearden or Dave Scott—are talkers. *Quiet* isn't a word you'd use to describe any of them.

Matt was different. Matt was an observer, someone who clearly liked to hover on the sidelines of group scenes and take his time getting a read on everything. He was like this, according to his family, even as a kid. Whenever he went into a new situation, he would hang back and take his time to observe before stepping in and getting involved. People sometimes got the impression that he was shy, but that wasn't it. He just liked to get the lay of the land. He liked to think before he leaped.

Matt looked a good deal like Paul Newman and had that same affable, good-natured personality that made him impossible not to like. (He also shared Newman's passion for cars and car racing. Matt's '69 Corvette was one of his most prized possessions, and his dad had a Triumph TR6 at home that the two were planning to rebuild together.) At the sniper course, Matt consistently shied away from the usual ball-busting locker room SEAL antics, and anytime someone else tried to give him any shit, he would simply decline to take the bait. Not that he couldn't have dished it right back if he'd wanted to. Something else I learned as I got to know him: The dude could think on his feet. His mind moved like lightning, and he could analyze a shooting problem in his head in half the time it took most students.

Another reason the other guys looked up to him was that he refused to judge others or participate in any kind of bad-mouthing. If anyone started complaining or cutting down someone else in the class, Matt would either find a way to change the subject or simply say, "Hey, let's not talk about that." And he was liked and respected enough by the other guys that he could get away with that, and instead of giving *him* shit they would go ahead and change the subject. I noticed that he spoke about others only in positive terms, and never gave voice to a person's vices or flaws—a character trait that so impressed me, I soon found myself emulating it.

Matt and Morgan reminded me of Glen and me when we first arrived at sniper school. They were new guys, as Glen and I had been, and they were obviously close friends. I soon learned that the two had gone through BUD/S together, were paired up as swim buddies in second phase, and were not just good friends but *best* friends. Despite being a study in contrasts, they made a great pair. Or maybe it was in part *because* they were a study in contrasts. Morgan grew up in Houston, a Texas boy through and through. We're talking conservative country here. Matt hailed from Cupertino, California, the heart of Silicon Valley. Temperamentally, too, they could hardly have been more different.

They not only clicked really well together, but they were also unswerving in the way they supported each other—unlike many of the other pairs, who would start getting on each other's nerves and barking at each other when the pressure got intense. Some guys would get pissed off and lose their cool if they lost a shoot or a stalk, and turn on their partners. When Matt or Morgan made a mistake, they'd just shrug it off and drive on with the mission. With some pairs the tensions escalated and friendships frayed as the course progressed. With Matt and Morgan, the bond grew only tighter.

Some of these students would get really frustrated when we would give them critiques, try to justify why they'd done it that way, explain what they were trying to do, or even talk us out of the critique itself. (To quote my daughter: *As if.*) Not Matt. With him there was no push-back; he would just listen carefully, saying nothing but, "Yeah," or, "Got it." He might nod, and you could see him taking mental notes. He would take it all in, then turn around and execute. You only had to tell Matt something once.

I quickly saw why Matt's platoon mates had given him the nickname Cool Hand Luke, and it wasn't just his resemblance to Paul Newman. It was that unshakable equanimity under pressure. People often use the phrase "quiet professional" to describe Navy SEALs and other Spec Ops warriors. I'd never met anyone who fit that phrase more perfectly than Matt. He had a level of competence that spoke louder than words.

Which goes to show that appearances *can* be deceiving—

even the most incisive first impressions. When I first met Morgan and Matt it seemed obvious that Morgan was the leader and Matt his sidekick. Watching them in action, I gradually realized that in many ways I'd gotten it backward: It was Morgan who often took his cues from Matt. Anytime Morgan would start getting frustrated, Matt had a way of glancing over at him without a word, just a look that said, *Pipe down and just get the job done.*

Matt knew my eyes were drilling holes in the backs of their heads, looking for any excuse to ratchet up the pressure even more—and he wasn't going to give it to me.

I soon learned that just because Matt was quiet didn't mean he was without pride. On the contrary, he had intensely high expectations for himself. For him, being a SEAL was more than an interest or pursuit. It was a deeply personal mission.

After high school Matt had enrolled in college to study political science and pursue his lifelong fascination with history. (Marcus, Morgan's brother, who was in the same SEAL platoon as Matt, described him as a bottomless font of knowledge about every culture, country, and population group, making him "our resident academic and Trivial Pursuit king.") After a few years at Cal State in Chico, Matt realized they couldn't deliver the degree course he wanted and transferred to San Diego, where he roomed with his brother, Jeff, and a few other guys—one of whom happened to be a SEAL.

Matt was also keenly aware of his own family's military history. His grandfather was career Navy and was stationed on the USS *Pennsylvania* at Pearl Harbor when the Japanese bombers attacked on December 7, 1941. Matt was stoked when he learned he'd been assigned to a unit stationed in Pearl City, because this meant he would be walking quite literally in his grandfather's footsteps. His grandmother was in the service, too, as were his father and uncle, who both served in Vietnam.

After college, degree in hand, Matt decided his career would have to wait. He told his parents, "I want to give back to my country first."

When I heard this I was impressed—and moved.

For a lot of us, joining the SEALs was something like joining the French Foreign Legion: the expression of a thirst for adventure. As Dave Scott said, "I get to shoot guns and jump out of planes . . . and get *paid* for it?" For me it was more the allure of being part of such an elite group. My teen years hadn't been easy, and I needed to prove to myself that I could do something of real worth. My decision to become a SEAL had not been driven by an especially strong sense of patriotism or, to be brutally truthful, even by the impulse to serve. For me the SEALs offered the chance to be part of something great, something special, to reach a level of achievement that put me among the best of the best. And as aspirational as that was, I also had to admit it was all about *me*, about what *I* wanted to experience and achieve.

Matt wasn't like that. Here was a kid determined to live his life as a gift, as an act of service to others. It certainly wasn't the first time I'd observed that quality. Mike Bearden was an outstanding example of a teammate I looked up to for his selflessness, and there were others. But with Matt that sense of devotion was so stark, it cut a deep groove in my consciousness.

Getting to know Matt affected me in two ways: First, it made me realize that over the course of my years in the teams, seeing the sacrifices so many guys and their families were making, and experiencing firsthand what was going on in the rest of the world, I'd come to have a deep love for my country, along with a dedication to serving that I hadn't known was in me.

He also made me want to up my game.

I was already fiercely dedicated to excellence, always had been. By natural inclination I have a very low tolerance for bullshit, laziness, or mediocrity. (One reason among many that Dave Scott and I clicked.) But just being around Matt and watching the way he held himself to the highest standard possible was pushing me to hold *myself* to an even higher standard. As much as our students looked up to us and took us as role models, every now and then it worked the other way, too. As Matt worked his way through the course, I found myself looking up to *him*. To me, he represented the epitome of what it was we were working to develop in all our students.

My favorite example of this is a story my buddy Dave Fernandez told me about an encounter he and Matt had later that year, a few months after Matt had been through our course.

That fall Matt's platoon was near the end of their predeployment workup and went through a set of final training exercises up in Bangor, Washington, which were led by Fernandez. Dave is a first-rate operator and he was hammering the piss out of these guys, getting them ready for their C1 certification. (C1 means you're combat-ready; C2 means you're not quite ready; C3 means you're not even close.) The platoon was what we call a "stacked platoon," meaning it was composed of all A-class operators. Despite that fact, unfortunately, the platoon was performing like shit. Or perhaps, as Dave points out, it was *because* they were all A-class operators and had trouble forming any kind of natural hierarchy that they were performing like shit.

Whatever the reason, they were doing a terrible job, and Dave had just pulled a training time-out. For a SEAL platoon on its final readiness exercises, this is unheard-of. Especially for Dave Fernandez.

"I am extreme about this," says Dave. "In conventional troop training, admin time-outs occur frequently as a safety measure. But in my book they have no place in SEAL training. If your platoon gets in a bind, tough. You're going to have to dig your own way out of it. That was my philosophy."

But these guys were such a train wreck, Dave was forced to call a halt and recall the entire platoon. They were running out of time, and he didn't want to have to flunk them. He reamed them out, told them where things stood, and directed them to regroup, get their heads in the game, start over, and this time make it work.

Dave and his crew were playing the role of the enemy, fitted out in indigenous garb and playing their part to the hilt. The platoon's task was to stay close enough to observe Dave's group but not be seen, and eventually make their way to shore and into the forty-degree water, where they would swim out to rendezvous with their recovery element.

Before long one of Dave's guys came to him and whispered that he'd located one of the men on the platoon. It was just going to dusk, and Dave had to peer carefully to see where his guy was directing him. Sure enough, there was a pair of steely blue eyes looking back at him. *Shit.* It was Axelson.

As Dave walked over to talk to Matt, he thought, *How the hell is this tall, curly-haired, blue-eyed, pale-skinned, Scandinavian-looking motherfucker ever going to blend in in the field?*

He knew Matt had a solid reputation, but he lit into him anyway. "As of right now you're on E and E"—escape and evasion, meaning he'd been spotted but not yet captured and would now have to escape. "Your ass is busted, I'm coming after you, and you'd better not let me catch you. It starts right now."

Without a word, Matt slipped back into the scenery as Dave went off to rally his team. Dave had been pulling for the platoon to pass, but now any reluctance to flunk them was gone. "I *want* this guy," he told his team. "I want his ass. Do not fail."

Now the platoon's fate rested on Matt's performance. Dave's team had a pretty good idea of what Matt would do and where he would go. He was headed for a rendezvous point whose location they all knew already. No matter how you sliced it, the odds were wildly stacked against him.

"And son of a bitch," says Dave. "I don't know how he did it. But he did it. That blond motherfucker just melted into the night. None of us ever saw him—and we knew exactly where he was going! Even at the end point, we never got a bead on him. Where the hell *was* that guy? It was the damnedest thing."

When Dave described the scene to me I laughed. I wished

Eric and I could take the credit for that feat. After all, the guy had just gone through our stalking course. But it wasn't just our course. It was Matt. He was one of the very best we had.

Which didn't mean he had an easy time of it in sniper school. Nobody does. Suffering is designed into it; that's the only way to create top-tier snipers. And those students soon learned that I wasn't kidding back in that Coronado bunker when I said they'd probably end up hating the course.

Since Pendleton is less than an hour's drive north of San Diego, Morgan would take off every evening and drive back down to Coronado, where he was rooming with his twin brother, Marcus, rather than stay at our barracks. Marcus remembers Morgan coming in every night, feeling exhausted and defeated. One evening he rolled in, collapsed on the living room couch, and said, "I am praying every night that they kick me out of this course. It sucks so bad. It's worse than BUD/S."

Marcus couldn't believe what he was hearing. He stared at his brother and said, "What are you talking about? *Nothing's* worse than BUD/S."

Morgan stretched out his long limbs, groaned, and said, "Man, it's a different kind of suck."

Marcus could not wrap his head around this. "What do you mean, 'a different kind of suck'? I'm a SEAL; I know what the definition of 'suck' is." A few months later, when he went through the course himself, Marcus understood exactly what his brother was talking about. "Please, God," he remembers muttering, "let them kick me out of this frigging course—I can't stand it!"

Matt was having just as hard a time as Morgan. His mother remembers him calling home one day and saying, "Oh, man, I only got a sixty percent today. I've *got* to get my average higher if I want to make it through this course!" He was consumed with worry that he was going to flunk out.

I understood why he felt so much anxiety about it. Every sniper student did. But he had no reason to worry. At no time was he ever at serious risk of failing. He and Morgan ended up finishing at the top of their class.

As I said, observing the way Matt held himself to the highest standard possible goaded me to hold *myself* to an even higher standard. I didn't know it then, but within months this would push me into one of the riskiest decisions of my years on the teams. In fact, it would take me within a hairbreadth of ruining my career.

When September came, Matt and Morgan returned to their platoon, and Eric and I were on to our next class of new students. Except that it was *not* business as usual. Axelson's presence in the course that summer had hammered home an ironic fact about our sniper course that was gnawing at me and making my life increasingly miserable. It had to do with *my* mentor.

Throughout my time in the Navy I saw striking examples of good leadership, mediocre leadership, and terrible leadership. When it was good, it was life-changing. Nobody exemplified that more than Bob Nielsen, our division officer.

In the short time we worked together, Bob was a tremendous role model and mentor for me. We talked every day, not only about the changes in the course and how that was going, but also about my life and my career. Bob knew that sooner or later I had a decision coming: whether to continue working as an instructor; or try out for a top-tier unit, as he had done; or get out of the service altogether. This fork in the road wouldn't come for a few years yet, but I was thinking about it. Bob knew that, and he served as a wise and solid sounding board.

The greatest thing about working for Bob was that he completely empowered us to run his course. "You guys are it," he told us. "You're the experts; I trust you." When someone you look up to and respect so highly puts his trust in you and gives you the mandate to act, that's the greatest feeling in the world. Our hard work made Bob look good—and in fact, that was a big part of our motivation. We *wanted* to make him look good.

But Bob wasn't the problem that was gnawing at me now. The problem was that Bob wasn't there anymore. When I said, "In the short time we worked together," I meant it. Barely a month after Eric and I arrived at the course, Bob called me into his office and let me know he was moving on to another billet. Then he told me who his replacement would be: a master chief named Harvey Clayton.

"*Harvey?* Shit, Senior Chief Nielsen! You have to be kidding me." I knew Master Chief Clayton by reputation, and it wasn't a good one. He was a dyed-in-the-wool fleet Navy guy who'd come to the teams as a senior enlisted man with no real experience downrange. He'd made chief right away and been shuffled around the teams in a variety of admin roles. I'd been fleet Navy myself for four years before joining the SEALs and, as I knew firsthand, they are two completely different cultures. And while he was a hell of a shot and an excellent match shooter, match shooting is not sniping, and Harvey had no real-world experience as a sniper. Putting someone like that in charge of a group of SEALs would be like trying to work inch-based nuts and bolts with a metric toolkit.

On top of which, I'd heard he was a major dick to work for.

Bob gave me a bland, unreadable look. "I know this course will be in good hands with you guys," he said. "No doubt in my mind." He clearly knew that Harvey was a poor choice for the position, but he just as clearly trusted Eric and me, and figured that however difficult Harvey might be, he would at least stay out of our way. "Sorry, gents," Bob said.

I don't think he ever dreamed just how bad it would get.

Harvey's deficiency as a sniper should not have been a problem, in and of itself. All he really had to do was lean on us. Between Eric and me and our other instructors, we had it completely covered. Things might have worked out fairly well if he had just let us do our jobs. The problem was, he was incredibly insecure toward junior, more experienced instructors, and that insecurity just would not let him get out of the way and allow us to do what we were there to do. Once he took command, it quickly became obvious that our working relationship was the opposite of what we'd had with Bob Nielsen. Whereas Bob would defer to us, with Harvey everything had to be his idea. It had to be his course, his curriculum. And he was strongly resistant to most of the very innovations that Eric and I were trying to implement.

If Bob Nielsen exemplified the best in leadership, Harvey was leadership at its most abysmal. He micromanaged the teaching and curricula, was patronizing and antagonistic to students, and exercised poor judgment in countless decisions both large and small. The quality of the course began to suffer as a result. We'd made Bob look good. Harvey was making *us* look terrible.

Harvey's behavior had been a problem during that summer session with Matt and Morgan. After they graduated and we moved into the fall, things grew even worse.

That fall was the last time we held the course at Camp Pendleton. Nailing down a consistent, established location for the shooting portion of the course had been a constant headache, and as much as we wanted it to, Pendleton wasn't working out. This was a Marine facility, which meant we didn't have priority. We'd reserve the range, but the Marines could kick us out whenever they wanted.

The rifle club several hours to the north where Glen and I had gone through the course in 2000 was another possibility. In fact, this was an ideal location in many ways. But there was one big problem with that place. The dry, dusty environment harbored *coccidioidomycosis* ("valley fever") spores. This didn't seem to bother the locals; maybe they'd adapted to it. When out-of-towners came for an event that might last just a few days, they didn't seem troubled by it. But living out there in tents for weeks on end, our guys kept getting sick, and valley fever can be brutal. As much as I loved that location, I'd had to face the fact that we just couldn't use it.

Except Harvey disagreed.

"We're going to make it work," he said. "We'll do dust mitigation—get a water truck up there and spray it down every day." *Right*, I thought. *Like that'll work.*

In every class, the senior (i.e., highest-ranking) student

serves as class leader. That session our class leader was Rob, a guy I knew from Team Three. Rob came to me and said, "Hey, Instructor Webb, we got our teams to pay for trailers. We're going to rent RVs so we don't have to sleep in the tents and inhale all that toxic dust."

I thought Rob's solution was brilliant. Harvey didn't.

"Absolutely not!" he said when he heard what the students were planning. "That's a waste of the Navy's money! I've got the water truck lined up, and it won't be a problem." He put the kibosh on the whole thing—called their command and had them cancel the RVs. I was furious. There was no reason to pull the plug on this plan. It would have been no skin off Harvey's back; the money was coming out of Team Three's budget. Whether it was Harvey's need to show he was in control or just plain meanness, it was unconscionable.

But wait. It got worse.

There we were: up in that spore-infested environment again, no trailers, the guys putting up their tents to get ready for the course. First day of the session, guess who shows up in a fucking RV? If you guessed Harvey, you'd be right. During the six long weeks of that shooting phase he was the only one there who was not sleeping in a tent. And of course his spraying-down-the-dust plan was worthless. To no one's surprise (but Harvey's) our guys started getting sick again. It was an abomination.

Harvey's behavior went from bad to worse. Now he started getting drunk, stalking the facility and yelling at the students he didn't like. It was beyond embarrassing.

When the students were given course critiques to fill out, they hammered him, calling him "unprofessional," "hurting credibility," and "a clear weak point" in the course. One of them wrote, "Master Chief Clayton is an idiot." I watched Harvey turn crimson as he read through them. He grabbed a handful of the papers and said, "I'm going back in there, and they're going to fill these out all over again!"

"Master Chief Clayton," I explained, "you can't do that. These are their fucking critiques! The whole point is to get their honest feedback."

He glared at me, stalked out of the office, went back into the classroom, and ordered the students to fill out new critiques. (Which they did—and they filled them out exactly the same way again.)

Three of our instructors were newly minted chiefs themselves. I went to them and said, "Guys, we have to do something about Harvey. It can't go on like this. He's killing the course."

They knew I was right. They also knew my hands were tied. I was in charge of the course—but I wasn't a chief.

In the Navy, the title of chief refers to the upper ranks of enlisted men. Becoming a chief is a serious accomplishment. Chiefs are the Navy's version of senior management. They have their own eating area on the ship (called the chiefs' mess) and walk their own walk. Even officers (if they're smart, which they often are) will defer to a chief's judgment. In essence, chiefs run the Navy.

Harvey was a master chief, rank E-9. I was a petty officer first class, rank E-6. This problem was literally above my pay grade. If anyone was going to do something about the situation, it was going to have to be one of the three other chiefs; I knew it, and they knew it. Yet this was the last thing any of them wanted to do. In the military, going around your boss to complain about him to his superiors is one of the worst sins you can commit. But they also knew that Harvey was destroying the fabric and credibility of the course.

Finally one of our chiefs, Chris Sajnog, took it on.

And took it on the chin.

When Chris went to our command's master chief and complained about Harvey, the only impact it had was to get Chris knocked on his ass. He was instantly relieved of his post at the sniper course and went from the number one E-7 (chief) at the command to last. Any chance he had of ever making senior chief (E-8) evaporated on the spot. Chris had joined the Navy in the late eighties, graduated from BUD/S Class 199, and went on to a stellar career in the teams. He was at the top of his dive class and an excellent corpsman. Now his career was effectively gutted.

As Chris was cleaning out his desk, Harvey said to him, "Hey, Sajnog—no hard feelings."

Chris didn't say a word. "I wanted to crush his skull with my fist," he told me recently. But he held his tongue, and his fist. I don't know if I could have managed that level of restraint.

I had no appetite for dinner that night. Chris was gone, Harvey reigned supreme, and I had nothing to show for our attempted coup but a large knot in my stomach. I didn't see how things could get any worse. I went back to my office in our subterranean bunker and sat in my desk chair, brooding. There was nothing I could do. With Chris thrown under the bus, there was no way either of the other two chiefs were going to risk making a move. Not being a chief myself, I was clearly powerless in this situation.

And then, out of the blue, I thought about Matt Axelson.

By this time Matt was long gone from sniper school, off

somewhere with his platoon in their final training and preparation before deploying to Afghanistan. But the impact of watching him go through our course had stayed with me, and now, as I sat feeling sorry for myself at how royally Harvey had pissed on my life, I remembered something I'd witnessed the summer before, when Matt and Morgan were going through the course.

One day I was observing one of our instructors giving a group of students some training on how to take environmental factors into account when calling a shot. As I mentioned earlier, the fact that a metal rifle barrel expands as it heats up translates into increased pressure on the round as it passes through, which in turn means higher muzzle velocity and an altered arc of trajectory. Because of this, the instructor was explaining, you can't necessarily follow the specs from a DOPE sheet ("*data on personal equipment*," a table of shooting specs for your rifle). "The adjustment you made for elevation this morning may have worked perfectly this morning," he was telling the class, "but now it's a good twenty degrees warmer, and your round is going to have a proportionately flatter arc, so to compensate you need to adjust your elevation down—"

"No, no, no, no, *no!*" said Harvey, cutting the instructor off as he waded in. "Don't start changing your setting and messing everything up. Trust your DOPE, you guys, trust your DOPE!"

It was an appalling scene. Harvey had no interest in the kind of sophisticated ballistic know-how we were teaching; he was strictly old-school, and any newfangled ideas or significant improvements over what he'd learned when he was a student made him feel threatened. Which was bad enough.

But to butt in and contradict an instructor right in front of the students was so fundamentally inappropriate—and it was obvious that the students all knew that as well as I did. I could see it on their faces, their reactions to his hissy fit ranging from amused to incredulous to disgusted. Two or three guys standing behind Harvey who knew he couldn't see them actually rolled their eyes.

But not Axelson. Matt behaved with complete decorum. In fact, he was the only guy on the range that day giving Harvey his full attention. I knew damn well that *he* knew damn well what an ass Harvey was being. Matt was no fool, and he wasn't missing a beat. He was simply responding by being a total professional. Matt was being the grown-up here, and Harvey was being a child.

I vividly remembered standing there watching that scene unfold and thinking, *This is totally fucked-up.* That snapshot vignette had burned itself into my brain, and I couldn't erase it, forget it, or ignore it.

"Goddammit, Axelson," I muttered as I sat brooding in my bunker.

It was that higher-standard thing. No way around it. I would have to do this thing myself. Even if it meant throwing my career in the toilet, as Sajnog had done, the situation demanded it. If I didn't step up now, I wouldn't be able to live with myself.

"Goddammit, Axelson," I repeated, then got up from my chair, decision made. As long as someone like Harvey was in charge, we didn't deserve students like Matt.

I pulled together details of Harvey's bad behavior, took my collected papers to Harvey's superiors, and reported him.

Then held my breath all that night.

I don't know if it was the fact that I'd so carefully documented my claims, or that the warrant officer in charge decided to back me to the master chief he reported to, or that this was the second Harvey-related complaint in as many weeks. I'll likely never know. Whatever it was, by some miracle my point got through. The next day Harvey packed his bags and quietly left.

By the time the next session began, Harvey had left the Navy—and I'd made chief.

Over the next few months I got calls and e-mails from former students, thanking me for sticking my neck out (or to put it more accurately, for placing it directly on the executioner's block) and expressing their relief and gratitude that Harvey was finally gone.

I didn't say this to any of them then, but I'll say it now: They had Matt to thank.

June 28, 2005. It was a year, almost to the day, since I first saw Matt and Morgan standing in that bunker at Coronado at the induction of their sniper school class. During that year Morgan's brother, Marcus, had gone through the course, too, and just days after graduating he joined Matt and his platoon on the other side of the world. Now Marcus and Matt and two other teammates, Danny Dietz and Michael Murphy, were on a capture-or-kill mission in the Hindu Kush, going after a very bad dude variously referred to as Ben Sharmak or Ahmad Shah. Marcus and Matt would be the team's snipers, Danny and Mike serving as spotters.

The four men were positioned high up on a rocky mountainside, gazing down on the village where their target was reputed to be in hiding. After seven or eight miserable hours of trek-and-climb, they were dug in and prepared to be up on those hills above the village for days, maintaining invisibility and surveillance as they lay in wait, scratching what cloak of cover they could from the barren slope.

Suddenly Marcus froze at the sound of approaching footsteps. A small knot of goatherds was headed their way.

There's a sixth sense about the eyes. Scientists will tell you it's superstition; people will scoff at it as voodoo—but I've experienced it, and it's real. People can sense it when your eyes are on them. No matter how well concealed you are, if you train your eyes on someone nearby, you up the odds that he will glance in your direction. I don't know how it works; I just know it happens.

As the sound of footfalls cut into the silence of their mountainside hideout, every natural instinct screamed, *Look in the direction of the sound!*—but instead Matt instantly averted his eyes. The scant concealment available in the scrubby mountain foliage didn't give them much to work with. An impossible situation. Yet just as he had on that exercise going up against Dave Fernandez's team, Matt somehow pulled it off. He melted away. In the next instant the others saw and followed Axelson's example. All four men vanished.

"Those goat herders wouldn't have seen us at all," says Marcus, "if it weren't for the fact that they happened to be walking straight toward us."

But the little group was practically on top of them now, and confrontation was inevitable.

What happened next is the subject of Marcus's book (and

the Peter Berg film adaptation) *Lone Survivor*. Faced with the decision of whether or not to quietly execute the three goat herders on the spot to keep their own location secure, the team made the excruciating choice to let the three go and hope for the best. Within minutes their mission was compromised and the four were fighting for their lives against impossible odds. Only one—Marcus—would make it out alive.

In a situation like this critical factors and complications start multiplying instantly, far too fast for linear thought to be of any use. Ninety-nine people in a hundred would panic or freeze. Matt never lost his cool, not for a fraction of a second. Marcus describes him leaning calmly up against a rock, in complete control and without a wasted movement or squandered round, acquiring target after target and getting off each shot with unerring accuracy.

A firefight is a messy, chaotic, nightmarish experience. Even five or six seconds of this rapidly exploding lethal chaos feels like an hour and has an impact on your psyche that stays with you the rest of your life. But this battle on the harsh Afghanistan mountainside didn't last five or six seconds; it raged on and on and on. Estimates of the enemy's number have ranged from several dozen to several hundred, but whatever it was, the four SEALs were badly outnumbered and outgunned.

Shot in the head and chest, Matt continued fighting to protect his buddies. Despite his mortal wounds he willed himself to hold out as long as his ammunition did, and longer, continuing on a good distance despite his wounds. Marcus recalls that Matt had three magazines left when an RPG blast blew them apart, yet when they found his body nearly two weeks later, only one magazine remained and he was surrounded by piles of empty shells. I spoke with one of the medics who helped recover Matt's body. He said Matt's injuries were so extensive, it was amazing that he'd been able to cover any ground at all. He also had a bandage on one of his wounds, obviously self-applied. Right to the end he was stoically patching himself up so he could continue the fight and protect his brothers to his last breath.

Much has been written about Operation Red Wings. What goes mostly unsaid is that for many of us in the teams, it was a turning point. Between losing Matt, Danny Dietz, and Mike Murphy, and the sixteen others who perished in the effort to rescue them, it was the worst loss of life in a single day in the SEALs' forty-year history. A lot of us started questioning exactly what we were doing over there.

When Mike Bearden died I was fresh out of sniper school and had not yet been on my first deployment. I was a new guy, untested by battle. With 9/11 still a year over the horizon, there was no battle yet to test us. By the time Dave Scott fell to his death two years later, the world was at war and I'd been through not only the carnage on the USS *Cole* but also six bloody months in Afghanistan.

Things were pretty simple when my platoon first landed in Kandahar in the fall of 2001. The smoke had barely cleared over the World Trade Center complex. In addition to our platoon patch, we wore NYFD patches on our outfits. We knew why we were there and what we were doing. We were going to find the guys who did this and make them pay. What's more, we were going to track down and destroy the clandestine network of men and resources that had trained and armed these guys and were continuing to do so, as they prepared to wreak further destruction on America.

Things were pretty clear back then. But now, in 2005? It was four years later, another four years of being sucked that much deeper into the commitment and sacrifice of war. I was now a family man, a father of two, and the preciousness of life had new meaning for me.

Supposedly we had rooted out the Taliban and quashed the al Qaeda influence there. But our guys were still over there, and things were not looking any better. For every ten hostiles we took out, a hundred more sprouted up. The restrictive ROEs that we were so glad we didn't have to follow on the USS *Cole* (and that did not exist when we first landed in Afghanistan in 2001) were now back with a vengeance, smothering our guys in the field. The administrative machinery that ran Spec Ops was starting to bloat, and effective tactical and strategic decisions on the ground were starting to feel the suffocating force of political considerations in the comfortable corridors of Washington. We were graduating the best combat snipers and Spec Ops warriors in U.S. military history and had become excellent at winning battles. But to what end?

When Harvey was my boss I had risked my career to make sure we had a sniper course that deserved guys like Matt. Now I was starting to wonder whether we had a war that deserved guys like him.

In November 2012, I brought my nine-year-old daughter, Madison, with me to New York for a week. In between meetings with publishers and media people, we would slip in all kinds of sightseeing, and it would be a fantastic chance for building some father-daughter memories. The first thing we did, though, even before leaving the West Coast, was to drive up to San Francisco to participate in a Veterans Day event hosted by Donna Axelson, Matt's mother, in Cupertino.

After Matt and his teammates died, the city of Cupertino commissioned a lifelike bronze statue, by the renowned Florida sculptor W. Stanley Proctor, to be erected at Memorial Park, which up to that point, oddly enough, had no memorial. Designed to commemorate all veterans, the statue itself is of Matt and his close friend James Suh, who was one of the sixteen men who died in the helo crash trying to rescue Matt and his friends. (You can see it online at CupertinoVeterans Memorial.org.) Around the base of the pedestal are placed twenty twelve-by-twelve-inch pavers, one for each of the nineteen men who died in Operation Red Wings, with their birth dates and dates of death, plus one for Marcus, which reads simply, "Survivor."

Donna holds an annual event there, where she talks about what the memorial means to her and to all of us. Each year she invites guest speakers to join her. That year she had invited me.

I talked about Matt and his buddies Danny Dietz and Mike Murphy, and the nature and meaning of their sacrifice. I retold a story by Marine Lieutenant General John Kelly, called "Six Seconds to Live," about two young Marines who gave their lives standing down a suicide bomber in Iraq, and how much that story reminded me of Matt and his teammates. (If you haven't heard the "Six Seconds" story, it's worth searching it out on the Internet.) Most of all, I spoke about what amazing men these three were, and how I was a better man for having known them.

Madison sat in the front row, right next to Donna, throughout my talk. Afterward people came up to her, thanking her and telling her how much my talk had meant to them. After the whole thing was over and we were alone together, she looked at me and said, "Dad, I'm really proud of you." I've seen a lot of good and a lot of bad in my years on earth. Among the mix there have been some outstanding moments. That one ranks right up there at the top.

Months later Madison was still talking about that experience. I hadn't realized it would have such an impact on her. But of course it did. If anyone tells you that children can't handle the realities of life, that they can't grasp the truth of life and death, you can tell them, "Sorry, but you don't know what you're talking about." My daughter's life was changed forever by hearing about Matt and his teammates. Although she never met him, she'll never forget him.

My hope is that the same will be true for her entire generation. Matt exemplified the simple truth that actions speak louder than words. Much like that Stanley Proctor bronze, Matt's life stands as a mute but eloquent monument to the best and noblest impulses within us all.

VISIONARY

JOHN ZINN

In July 2006, eighteen months after making chief and wrestling command of the NSW sniper course from Harvey Clayton's hands, I left the U.S. armed services and faced the question every Spec Ops warrior must face sooner or later: *What now?* Once you've trained for years to become part of the world's most elite fighting force, then spent long stretches in the thick of some of the most dangerous conflicts on the globe, what do you do for an encore?

Getting out of the service wasn't an easy choice. I had put in nearly fourteen years of active service in the Navy. Sticking it out for another six would buy me a decent retirement package. I had colleagues who couldn't believe I would even think about walking away with only a few years to go. Some were actually angry at me, which surprised me. (What did they think, I was somehow letting them down?) But I'd put the Navy and the teams ahead of my wife and kids for too many years.

Marriage and being part of the teams is not an easy mix. The day our first child was born I was in the Persian Gulf, headed for terrorist hideouts in the caves of Afghanistan. I didn't even meet my son until he was six months old. When our second came along I was constantly on the road, developing and teaching advanced courses to sniper students, and those long months away were tough on our relationship. The birth of our third was only weeks away, and I was worried that our marriage was being pulled to the breaking point.

It was time to put family first. I had to leave the teams.

The question was, and do what?

For a lot of us in the Spec Ops world, it can be a tough transition. After years of being either in combat or in training for combat, it feels strange to conform to the dictates and behaviors of the civilian workplace. It's not necessarily hard to *get* work; there are plenty of private-sector firms who are anxious to hire people with the knowledge, experience, and skill sets of a Navy SEAL. It's just hard to adapt to what others think of as a "normal" work situation.

We typically don't make very good employees. Regular soldiers and sailors are trained to work well as functioning parts of the collective, good cogs in a larger watchworks. In the SEAL teams you're not taught simply to obey orders; you're taught to accomplish the mission, however that works and whatever it takes. We are groomed to think fast, think for ourselves, and think unconventionally. If soldiers and sailors are the military's version of a solid corporate workforce, we are its entrepreneurs, innovators, and misfits.

If I was going to leave the employ of the government, the only employer I was interested in going to work for was myself. With a family of five to feed, that was a daunting prospect, but I couldn't see doing it any other way.

Fortunately for me, I had some excellent role models. And one in particular.

. . .

I met John Zinn in the late nineties, when we had both just completed our respective BUD/S classes and joined Team Three. I was standing in the middle of a class on advanced diving techniques while our instructor gave a safety brief, something about how to avoid getting sucked into giant turbines and turned into fish food, when I heard a Clint Eastwood voice rasp quietly behind me: "Everyone has to die someday. . . ." I craned my neck just enough to look back, half expecting a scowling Man with No Name chewing on a cheroot. Instead I found myself eyeballing a cherub-faced towhead cracking a faint smile. (A piece of human nature trivia I learned in the teams: The more time a guy spends in the water, the drier his sense of humor.)

John and I were both southern California surfers, and we hit it off right away. If your picture of a Navy SEAL is a big, chiseled, pro-football type with rippling muscles and a fuck-you glare, then you never would have pegged John for a SEAL. A slender five-eleven, with sandy blond hair, an oval face, an affable smile, and quiet confidence, he looked like your average skinny surf bum.

John was a competitive swimmer almost before he could walk. His first swim meet, at age five, was abysmal. The other kids dived into the water and swam to the end of the pool and back before John had even touched the other side. That was it for John: He never lost a meet again, and that capacity to take fuel from failure would become his signature gift.

The water was John's passion and driving force. An excellent athlete, he played competitive water polo throughout his school years. During his senior year of high school his dad took him to become scuba-certified, and John was so far ahead of everyone else in the tests that the instructors started calling him Neptune. He could have gone on to university on a water polo scholarship. But he wanted more than anything to join the Navy and become a SEAL. Four days after his high school graduation, he was on his way to Great Lakes, Illinois, to attend Navy boot camp. He was barely seventeen. A year and a half later he was starting BUD/S.

John had no illusions about how tough the selection process would be, but he was determined to make it through no matter how hard it got. Of course, nobody goes into BUD/S *planning* to fail. Your first day on that asphalt grinder at Coronado you hear everyone around you saying, "Hey, man, no way *I'm* quitting!" And a few days later, as you drag yourself out of your bunk in the frigid predawn darkness, bruised and battered and beaten, and you hear the morning silence split by the bone-jarring *clanggg, clanggg* of that damn brass bell, you know another sorry-ass motherfucker has thrown in the towel. My class started with 220 candidates; by graduation seven months later there were twenty-three of us left. It's easy to talk a big game, but when the reality of BUD/S starts to sink in, people crumble. Not John. He was so focused, so intent on plowing through and going straight into the SEALs, that it was impossible to imagine him *not* doing it.

And yet, just as with that first swim meet at age five, his first time out he *did* fail.

BUD/S Class 205 began in December 1995. It was near the tail end of a record-length El Niño surge, and major storms were pummeling California. By the time they reached Hell Week, it was one of the coldest on record. John ended up with pneumonia and was forced to call a halt.

Getting rolled from BUD/S just about killed him. Not the

pneumonia—the blow to his ego. He wasted no time on self-recrimination, though. That fuel-from-failure thing again. It wasn't the first time he'd suffered a bitter defeat on the way to triumph, and it sure as hell wouldn't be the last.

There's a common idea in the SEALs that says, if you don't make it through BUD/S on your first try, you need to go out and get some experience before you come back for a second shot at it. John decided to take a turn as a naval police officer. He wangled an assignment to Lackland Air Force Base in San Antonio to go through a six-week training course, and upon graduating was assigned to police duty at the naval station in Guantánamo Bay, Cuba. After eighteen months of breaking up bar fights and keeping the peace, he showed up back in Coronado, ready to do BUD/S again. This time he went the distance, and graduated Class 217 in mid-'98, just a few months after I finished Class 215.

As new guys at SEAL Team Three, John and I went surfing together as often as we could. We also shared an aspiration to become successful in business, and during our time together at Team Three we talked a lot about being entrepreneurs and all that we wanted to accomplish in our lives.

At the time I had begun investing in real estate and having some modest success, to the extent that I owned my own home and rented out a guesthouse on the property. I'd studied Robert (*Rich Dad, Poor Dad*) Kiyosaki's approach to building a portfolio of income-generating assets, and I was convinced real estate was the way to go.

John wasn't especially interested in real estate. He wanted to build something. He wanted to create and run his own business. Actually, that's not saying it right: He didn't just *want* to run his own business—it was more like a burning, all-consuming drive. He *had* to.

Right away I noticed that John had a distinctive quality of absolute confidence. When he talked about something happening in the future, it was so vivid, so real, you *knew* it would happen. A common experience for SEALs is that, once having been part of this incredibly elite team, it can seem impossible to imagine that any other experience could come close, as if the path of achievement were by definition downhill from there on. That wasn't John's view at all. "I have bigger fish to fry," was how he saw it. And he was 100 percent positive that he would build something that would become hugely successful.

Figuring out exactly what that would be . . . that was another story.

In the spring of 2000 he asked his lawyer father, Michael, to help him form his own corporation as part of a plan for a restaurant that incorporated a gigantic man-made wave, so that people could come to the restaurant and surf while they were there. He became interested in buying the rights to a British-made amphibious vehicle and distributing it here in the States. He tried his hand at stockbroking. It became a running joke at Michael's office: John calling and yet again changing his articles of incorporation to fit his latest new idea. Over the next few years that corporation's name would change six times—and there were dozens of other business ideas that never even made it to the corporate-naming stage. Nothing quite came together. To a casual observer, John's serial-entrepreneur efforts might have seemed no more than a string of harebrained ideas that would never amount to anything. It would be a few years before the evidence proved it, but that casual observer would have been dead wrong.

Meanwhile John and I had continued in our SEAL careers on parallel tracks. When I went to Golf Platoon he joined Bravo, our sister platoon, and deployed to the Middle East at the same time we did. While we were part of the amphibious readiness group (the one that ended up rushing to the aid of the stricken USS *Cole*), Bravo was stationed in Bahrain, where they engaged in noncompliant ship boardings, enforcing UN sanctions against Iraq. On that deployment John proved himself one of their team's most outstanding performers.

A hostile ship boarding, called a VBSS (visit, board, search, and seizure), is a high-speed, precision operation. After sneaking up alongside the hostile ship with your fast boats, you have to get your guys up and over the ship's railings before the onboard crew of smugglers and pirates even realizes you're there, because the moment they know they're being boarded they'll take aggressive countermeasures. In the case of a smuggling ship on the Gulf, they'll haul ass for nearby Iranian waters, where you're legally powerless to do anything.

During the critical split-second *board* phase of one of Bravo Platoon's VBSS operations, one of the guys fired a grappling hook that failed to catch on the pirate ship's railing.

"I was still processing the fact that the thing hadn't taken," John's OIC explained afterward, "and in a fraction of a second John threw another hook up there by hand." John's hook caught, and within the next few seconds he had scuttled up the line and was up there on the railing laying down suppressing fire with a squad automatic weapon (SAW) while the rest of the boarding team crawled up the line after him. "I'd never seen a reaction time like that before," his OIC added. "And I've never seen one since."

When our deployments ended, John and I were both coming up for reenlistment, which would mean a decent cash bonus if we opted to stay in. I was married by this time, John was engaged to his girlfriend, Jackie, and we were both thinking about the financial demands of starting a family. I took the bonus and stayed in, moving from Golf to Echo Platoon, which was scheduled to go overseas later that year (though we could hardly have guessed we would end up in the mountains of Afghanistan hunting for terrorist training camps). John took a different path. When Bravo Platoon got back from their deployment at the end of 2000, John surprised Jackie by saying he wasn't going to reenlist. He loved being part of the teams—but he wanted out.

John was a valuable asset (he was hell on the M60 machine gun), and our command didn't want to lose him. The commander of SEAL Team Three offered to raise his bonus, but John turned him down. The offer went up; he turned it down again. They finally got up to sixty thousand dollars (an unheard-of amount), but he turned that down, too.

As he said, he had bigger fish to fry.

John left the service in early March 2001, and he and Jackie were married a few weeks later. By this time Jackie had her master's degree in food science and had gotten a good job offer from National Food Laboratories, up in the San Francisco Bay Area. Since John had enlisted right out of high school, Jackie suggested he take this opportunity to go back to school and get a degree. "I grew up on the East Coast," she says, "in a family where it was ingrained into us that the way to success was to go to college and get a good job. I really couldn't picture any other path." John didn't see it that way, and he didn't give much of a damn about school, but he agreed to give it a shot. They moved to the Oakland area and he enrolled in a community college there while he looked for a job.

John found college life frustrating and at times infuriating. The other students were only a few years younger than he was, but to John they seemed like kids who had seen nothing of real life. It was hard to sit there listening to those professors spouting their academic worldviews, armchair-quarterbacking events halfway around the world—events John had seen up close in all their gritty reality. While I was tracking down Taliban and al Qaeda forces in the mountains of Afghanistan, John was sitting in a classroom being bored out of his mind.

Meanwhile, he continued coming up with idea after idea for new businesses. Every time he hatched a new concept he'd pitch it to Jackie, who listened and did her best to temper her own natural skepticism. Earlier that year, just before they were married, John had presented Jackie with the idea of putting ex–military personnel on domestic passenger flights. "Our biggest national threat is in the air," he told her. He changed his corporation's name to SkyGuard and worked with a martial arts master to develop a simplified version of Okinawan karate that flight attendants could employ in the narrow confines of a passenger airplane aisle, with a curriculum they could cover in about two hours.

Jackie had thought the idea was a bit far-fetched. Then 9/11 happened. "Oh, my God," she told him. "You were right!"

Still, the SkyGuard idea did not come together. Jackie adored John and believed in him. But so far none of his brilliant ideas had panned out—and they had to eat. John needed to get a job.

Toward the end of 2001 John got a job offer with the sheriff's department in Half Moon Bay, a sleepy San Francisco suburb. With eighteen months as a naval police officer in Guantánamo Bay, plus four years in the SEALs, he was the very definition of "overqualified." Be that as it may, the job required that he enroll in a five-month program at the police academy there. He started in January 2002.

John was the best student his instructors had ever seen at the academy, both physically and academically. Which was interesting, considering that John had never before been more than a mediocre student (unless the subject involved athletics). But over his years in the service he had learned how to focus his energies on whatever task he saw as important, and he was killing their standards. The jock who didn't care about school had become the ultimate student.

One week before graduation, the cadets were practicing one-on-one takedowns. John was disgusted at how laid-back his classmates were as they went through the motions. When his turn came and a classmate faux-attacked him, John took the guy down for real, and hard. He didn't injure the man, but that dude was *down* before he had a clue what had hit him.

The instructor suspended John on the spot. After a hasty conference, the administration judged him "too aggressive" for the academy. With a week to go till graduation, he was booted out of the program.

John was devastated. He could joke about it to Jackie ("I would've been better off over in Oakland, where there's a murder every day!"), but it was no joke. Being kicked out of the academy also meant the police job was gone. The young couple had just bought a home and were now carrying a substantial mortgage. Jackie's job notwithstanding, they really needed John to generate an income.

This was the spring of 2002, and the so-called War on Terror was just hitting its stride. My platoon was on its way home from Afghanistan, to be replaced by others. Things were already heating up in Iraq, and those on the inside could sense the drumbeat to war. The government was stepping up its use of contract security agents overseas. As part of Team Three, John's AO (area of operations) in the SEALs had been the Middle East, so he was highly qualified. If the Half Moon Bay police department couldn't see a way to use him, private security companies like DynCorp and Blackwater sure could. And the money was good.

So John signed up, and for the next few years he was in and out of the Middle East, working as a private contractor.

In the summer of 2002, when Hamid Karzai became president of Afghanistan's interim government, John was there as part of his security detail. A year later, as the dust settled in Iraq from the U.S.-led Shock and Awe campaign, John was there sweeping the country for WMDs. When L. Paul Bremer became in effect the interim chief executive of Iraq, John was on hand, guarding him as well.

Those years were a terrifying time for Jackie. It seemed to her that every night there was news about yet another roadside bomb in the Middle East—and all she could do was hope

John was nowhere near it. She was right to be terrified, because there were in fact times when he was quite near the action indeed.

Especially one pivotal day in late January 2004.

By 2004 the situation in Iraq had seriously deteriorated and was getting more dangerous by the day. John and an ex–Green Beret buddy, Ron Griffin, would spend each day hazarding the streets of Iraq, then get together in the evenings to talk over what they'd seen during the day and discuss the tactical failures they'd witnessed.

One major source of problems lay in the vehicles they were driving, which were typically some sort of high-end SUV, retrofitted with armor plating. The problem was that everyone on the street knew who was in these vehicles, because nobody over there but Americans was driving those models. Our guys might as well have had neon signs saying, "We're Americans! Shoot at us!" The bad guys would stand up on overpasses with binoculars, scope out one of these cars, and suddenly you're getting an RPG up the tailpipe. (Ron called them "to whom it may concern shots.")

And it wasn't only a matter of how recognizable the cars were. These vehicles just weren't designed for the punishment they were taking. John and Ron were constantly wrestling with fuel-incompatibility issues, suspension system failures, problems with doors, windows, and other secondary electromechanical systems, and all sorts of mechanical fuckups. Under normal circumstances failures like these would be minor annoyances. In conditions of urban combat they could be catastrophic.

"If someone doesn't do something about these vehicles," John said to Ron, "we're going to lose a lot of our guys."

On January 27, 2004, John was part of a convoy on a mission through the mean streets of the city where he and Ron were working. No matter how skillful the driving or how well the three drivers kept their distance, there was no way their vehicles could not stand out like three-piece suits in an inner-city street fight. Sure enough, the convoy was ambushed. The vehicles in front managed to escape the kill zone and get away, leaving John and his companions in the hot seat. A slew of hostiles came up from behind, and John and his buddies' car started taking heavy fire. According to the after-action report, armor-piercing rounds were fired into the vehicle through their windows. Manning the machine gun in back, John returned fire out the shattered back windshield while the driver practiced every evasive tactic he knew.

Which was when one of the vehicle's "safety" features nearly got them killed.

A grenade blew up under the chassis, severing one of the car's brake cables and causing the vehicle to lock up and come to an instant and complete stop.

"Motherfucker!" the driver said. John's only comment was another volley from the big gun.

Back at base, Ron was having lunch when he and a few other guys heard the calls coming over: "Contact! Contact! Contact! . . ." Ron and the others jumped into two cars to form an immediate reaction force, get out there as quickly as possible, and pull out any survivors.

Meanwhile, their vehicle immobilized, John and his two

teammates had no choice but to hoof it. John continued shooting out the back of the car, laying down enough cover fire so the other two guys could start moving out before he quit and joined them. When you're shooting an automatic weapon in an enclosed space, it isn't kind to your hearing. And John did not go light on bullets. From that day on he was deaf as a post in his right ear.

The three went on foot now, winding their way through some back streets until they found a friendly cabbie who stopped and turned over his car keys to them. They thanked the man, hopped in, and quickly realized the cabbie hadn't done them much of a favor: The damn thing was on its last legs. They made it another quarter of a mile before the cab quit on them.

Back on foot again. Eventually they found a junkyard area they could slip into and get some concealment. They holed up there until one of the two reaction vehicles caught up to them and got them out.

Once back at base they learned that, by some miracle, we had not lost a single one of our men in the attack.

John and Ron stayed in-country until March, but that was their last trip as private contractors. That night they took a yellow legal pad and sketched out the concept for a vehicle that would become the focus of John's entrepreneurial energies from that point on.

"It's crazy over there," John told Jackie once he was back stateside. "Our guys are getting blown up left and right. What we need is a fully armored vehicle, built from the ground up to blend into the traffic of the country where we're operating."

Jackie heard the passion in his voice and saw the gleam in his eye. *Uh-oh*, she thought. *Here we go again*. But over the years she'd learned that John's business ideas, even though none had yet come to fruition, were often ingenious and at times brilliant. As John described the custom-built vehicle he envisioned, Jackie could see he was onto something important.

Not everyone had the same level of faith in the concept. After all, John and Ron were security guys, hired guns—not engineers. "Knuckle-draggers don't make vehicles," as Ron puts it. Well, that was about to change.

John wanted the vehicle to look indigenous and be as fully armored as possible without looking that way. *Indigenous. Armored*. He called up his dad with the seventh and final name for his corporation: Indigen Armor.

During the rest of 2004, while I was busy developing and teaching the NSW sniper course with Eric Davis, John and his partners (Ron and another ex–Spec Ops security guy) were creating Indigen Armor. They put together a detailed proposal, with CAD drawings of the vehicle they had in mind, then shopped their idea to companies with the connections and financial clout it would take to put it into production.

Every company they approached said the same thing: "Great idea—but we get pitched great ideas all the time. We're not interested until you actually build the thing and show it to us." Developing the *idea* for their vehicle was not going to cut it. They were going to have to hire someone to build them a working model of the damn thing.

John had already done the research and knew the ideal manufacturing partner. They approached a racing car company in southern California with a strong track record and a good-size manufacturing facility. The firm agreed to build their demo vehicle and be their manufacturing partner. All John and Ron had to do was come up with about a hundred thousand dollars. They each put in twenty grand themselves, money saved from their contracting work, and then did what every capital-deficient entrepreneur does: started talking to friends and family.

By July their financing was in place and they were ready to go. It took a little over two months to build their demo model, and John and Ron were on-site all day, every day. It was nerve-racking, having all that friends-and-family money on the line, and the 'round-the-clock intensity of the production process was brutal, even for guys who were used to working in a war zone. "Hellacious" is how Ron describes it.

That September they invited all the contacts they could come up with to a debut showing at the racing car company's facility in Huntington Beach. The showing was a runaway success. Soon they had a $10 million contract, starting with an order for four vehicles. John and his partners were able to pay back every investor—with interest—in far less than the promised one year.

Jackie's long-standing belief in John was vindicated at last: His dream company had become a reality. Indigen Armor was off and running.

Except that nothing ever goes according to plan. Ever. It's the first rule of combat, and the first rule of business.

One day John got a phone call from their client with some extremely upsetting news: The race-car company, their manufacturing partner, was going behind John's back. They wanted to squeeze Indigen Armor out of the picture altogether and deal directly with the client. After all, they were the ones building the thing, right?

In Special Operations you're trained to respond to any threat from any direction, no matter how unexpected, with immediate and decisive force. John and his partners didn't waste any time. They terminated their contract, sued the car company, and won a $2.1 million arbitration award. Which was good news financially—but now they were without a manufacturing partner, and where did that leave them? John was undaunted. Spec Ops training again: The ability to respond to any situation with creative solutions is just as important as knowing how to shoot your weapon. Often more so.

The day the wire transfer from the award landed in their corporate account, John said to Jackie, "Well, the Band-Aid's been ripped off." She asked him what he meant. He grinned and said, "It looks like we're gonna build these cars ourselves."

Jackie was floored. Was he saying they were going to create *their own production line*? John had never intended to become an automaker. He had no experience in designing, outfitting, or running a manufacturing plant. Was he out of his ever-loving mind?

But that was exactly what they did.

John had an uncanny ability to make things happen, sometimes seemingly out of thin air. I'll give you two of my favorite examples.

One day, when John was on a flight from D.C. to California, a child on his plane had a seizure. The boy had never had a seizure before and his mother had no idea what was happening. John, a trained EMT, immediately went into action, laid the boy out on his side and made sure his airway was clear, got a cool washcloth on his neck, and completely handled the situation—including keeping the boy's mother calm—until the boy was okay again.

Once everything had settled down, a man across the aisle leaned over and started talking with John. Clearly he was quite impressed with how the young man had handled himself. He handed over his business card and said, "If you ever need anything, don't hesitate to call me." Looking at the card, John realized the man was majority owner of a southern California bank. He laughed. "Funny you should say that," he replied. "There actually *is* something I need at the moment." What he needed was about half a million dollars to capitalize some major expansion in his plant.

The following week John was sitting in the man's bank, and a week after that he had secured a loan for half a million dollars. Michael said that in all his decades of practicing law, he'd never seen a business loan transacted from start to finish in so short a time, let alone one of that substantial an amount. John and the man from the plane ended up having a long and fruitful business relationship, with many millions more in financing along the way.

And the other example:

At one point John was touring potential clients through their production facility, showing their first-generation vehicle, which was a large sedan. He knew they needed to move into producing a next-generation run of smaller, Japanese-style vehicles, but they didn't have the funding for it yet. In the middle of the place he had set up a black box, and as they toured the plant, everyone kept eyeing the thing and asking, "What's in the black box?"

"We can't really show you that," John replied. "It's our next-generation concept, and it's amazing—but I'm afraid I can't tell you what it is just yet."

In fact, there was absolutely nothing in the box. It was empty. But that didn't matter. John completely sold them on the concept. Before long they had their financing, and their gen-two line was a complete success.

Today John's vehicles are used throughout the world. Indigen Armor can't release sales figures, but John's company has built a *lot* of vehicles—and saved a *lot* of lives. Over the years they received a constant stream of e-mails and notes like this one:

> I just wanted to write to thank you guys at Indigen Armor. I was on a mission today in the streets of the city where I'm stationed and our convoy was ambushed. The only reason I'm alive today is that I was driving one of your vehicles when it happened.

By 2008, John and his partners realized they had outrun their capacity to generate the kind of capital it would take to tool up to the full scope of operation John had in mind. It was time to sell. They shopped around and found a New York private-equity firm with a strong background in military and aerospace. They sold a majority interest in the business for a sizable sum, with John retained as president and CEO, in 2009—by which time I was already hip-deep in my own entrepreneurial deployment and being shot at from all sides.

. . .

When I left the service in mid-2006, Indigen Armor was already in full production and doing well, and I was inspired by John's example. But I didn't want to build vehicles; I wanted to train the guys who drove them.

John had wanted to build something. Me, I'd always been into real estate, even had my real estate license. My idea was to create a training facility somewhere in southern California that would serve both military and law enforcement personnel. I called it Wind Zero, named after a precision shooting term.

I had been thinking about this idea for years. I'd been out to Blackwater and other dedicated training facilities on the East Coast, and I knew from experience that there was nothing comparable on the West Coast. In fact, southern California was desperate for a solid, reliable training facility. At the sniper course we constantly had problems finding usable venues for our training. I would call units from other branches of the military and even local law enforcement units and ask, "Where are you guys going when you train?" Invariably the answer was, "We don't really know. We're doing our best to find whatever we can." The problem was systemic, and we were constantly having to ship guys out to other locations to train, which was both expensive and time-consuming.

There was a human cost, too: Sending people out of state for weeks and even months at a time was tough on their families. I'd experienced this myself. The strain those long stretches of absence had put on my own marriage was one of the driving reasons I'd made the decision to leave the teams. If we could provide a place where these young men and women could train during the day and be back home with their families at night, we'd be doing them a huge service.

I started developing the idea along with a fellow former SEAL, a Team Five guy named Randy Kelley, who had gotten out a year before me and started his own business training people in advanced security and surveillance techniques and technologies—something like Q in the James Bond movies (only with a North Carolina accent). Randy gave me free use of his office space and helped me write a business plan.

And it was one hell of a plan. In addition to shooting ranges, tracks for driving instruction, and indoor classroom space, Wind Zero would feature lodging and dining facilities for up to two hundred people. We would be able to embed actual buildings and cities that we could dress up so we could run large-scale urban-environment exercises, such as riot situations and other high-threat scenarios. We could facade the area out as an Afghan village this week, an urban downtown next week. The plan also included two helo pads and an airstrip.

In many cases we figured people would show up with their own trainers, such as law enforcement groups. We knew there would also be customers who would want us to provide the training. No problem. In fact, even as we were continuing to work on the facility itself, we put a training staff in place and started taking on contracts even without having our own facility in place yet.

Then we had the idea of adding more racetrack. There are a lot of car clubs in southern California, and some of them were telling us there was a huge market for motor sports. Porsche and BMW clubs approached us and said, "Hey, if you build it, we'll use it." So we bolted on a separate business to the original concept: a track where we could hold privately sponsored race car events. There would even be facilities where you could store your car in between events. An expert from the UK helped us design a full Grand Prix–style double track.

Now all I had to do was find and buy the land, get the full financing, and build it. The thing would cost something like $100 million all told.

Like John Zinn when he was first out of the service, in my first year out I took work as a private-contract security agent to pay the bills, which meant being over in Iraq for months at a time. In between those stints overseas I started combing southern California, looking for land. By the end of 2006 I had found the property I wanted, a thousand acres of raw land in Imperial County, not far from Niland, my old stomping grounds.

I was able to put down some option money from my savings and private-contract earnings, but that wouldn't hold the land for long. This was a $2 million–plus piece of real estate; the down payment alone would be north of three hundred thousand dollars. It was time to raise some serious investment.

At the same time, I set about the arduous process of securing entitlements.

In land-development terms, "entitlements" refer to the gamut of legal permissions and approvals you need in order to physically build the project. This can include zoning variances (or, in some cases, actual rezoning); land-use permits; approvals for roads, utilities, landscaping, and construction; and more. The process is slow, complicated, and frustrating.

For a project the size and scope of what we were planning, we figured it would probably take at least a year or two.

I had barely begun the process of developing Wind Zero when I found I had a serious competitor, the one private para-military training organization that everyone had heard of and had an opinion about: Blackwater.

When I was still on active duty I had bumped into some guys from Blackwater in Las Vegas at the annual SHOT (Shooting, Hunting, Outdoor Trade) Show, a major military/hunting industry trade event, and asked them why they hadn't done a West Coast facility yet. "The hell with California," they said. "It's too much of a pain in the ass." They must have since rethought this position, because by the time I put a contract on my Imperial County land, Blackwater had just come on the scene and was aiming to do the same thing.

I was there when they first rolled into town in their stretch Hummers, meatheads piling out with their Under Armour shirts that were two sizes too small and showed off every muscle fiber. It was obnoxious. They brought out a guy from the East Coast with a pronounced Boston accent and put him in charge of their project. First thing he told me when we met was how much he hated California.

I was determined to take the opposite approach.

As soon as I had our land picked out, I began building as much local support as possible. I took a year and a half getting to know the people there, spent time talking with the guys in law enforcement, the fire departments, and the rest of the public safety community, building relationships with them, telling my story and explaining the project. Once I had established a foundation of solid support, *then* I started going to the town's and county's political leadership and moving the entitlement process forward. I put twenty letters of endorsement from local community leaders in front of them, from the police chief to the community college president, and they said, "Holy shit, we had no idea we needed this kind of facility . . . but you know, it makes sense."

"Winning hearts and minds" isn't just a military strategy for working in foreign territory; it's common sense and common decency—and it works.

Two years after they started, the Blackwater effort crumbled under an onslaught of local opposition. There were anti-Blackwater bumper stickers everywhere. I knew it was over when I stepped outside one day and saw a lady walking her dog and wearing a T-shirt that said, "Stop Blackwater!"

Meanwhile our effort kept going. The entitlement process was even more complex, more difficult, more frustrating, and more drawn-out than our most conservative estimates. But we got through it. In December 2010, after four years of hard work, with millions of dollars on the line, we made it over the finish line and received official approval from Imperial County to build our facility.

It had taken four long years. We'd raised nearly $4 million and done it the hard way, piece by piece from more than forty different investors, with no angel investor forking over the lion's share. So many people had told me we would never get the entitlements. But we did. Where Blackwater had failed, we had succeeded.

The victory tasted sweet indeed—but it lasted just thirty days. Because nothing ever goes according to plan. Ever.

First rule of combat, first rule of business.

While I had strong support and no real opposition from the local community, there were forces working against me from other directions the whole time.

First there was Jack, a former SEAL I'd known from my deployment in Afghanistan. Jack had called me right at the start, before I even had my property, and tried to get me to back off. According to him, he was already planning to do something very similar himself. I suggested we both keep doing what we were doing and work together in a cooperative relationship. The demand was practically unlimited, I told him, and there was more than enough room for two training facilities in the marketplace. But Jack was one of those people who insists on trying to be the smartest guy in the room. (Me, I'd rather be the dumbest guy in the room. I have no problem working with people who are smarter than me—the more talented, the better.) He kept doing what he could to intimidate and discourage me and, when that didn't work, to sabotage me.

Then there was Casey, one of our investors, who had gradually taken on a more and more direct role in the project. Casey had more business experience than I did, and I looked up to him and tended at times to defer to him. My mistake. I gave him too much power in the company, and before long he was trying to edge me out altogether.

While I was battling these political and internal complications, the entitlement process had dragged on for what seemed like forever while the money we'd raised gradually dwindled to nothing. Eventually I had stopped taking a salary and started taking on consulting work here and there to keep the lights on.

At one point, just as I'd successfully fought off a mutinous takeover bid from Casey, we found ourselves battling a website that sprang up with the imposing name "Imperial Valley Against Wind Zero." Evidently there was a bitter groundswell of opposition from the local community . . . at least, that was what it was designed to look like. The truth, as we soon learned, was that nobody in Imperial Valley had anything to do with the website or its mission. In fact, it was an elaborate scheme concocted by Jack, my jealous ex-SEAL rival.

On the heels of the Stop Wind Zero site, an anti–Brandon Webb video appeared online, pasting together sound bites from my various media appearances and taking them out of context to make them look like I was saying things I'd never even remotely said. It was like one of those tacky political smear commercials you see proliferating on TV during every election cycle. Jack's handiwork again.

Still, we'd survived Casey, and survived Jack, and survived the exhaustion of our financial resources, and still managed to secure Imperial County's approval for our project.

And thirty days later the county was sued by the Sierra Club, who claimed that the environmental-impact study had not been sufficient. In fact, it was rock-solid, but that didn't seem to matter.

When I say "Sierra Club," that makes it sound like a large national groundswell. Actually it was a lone individual, a woman at the local Sierra Club chapter who was known for instigating frivolous lawsuits. The head of the planning commission had warned me about her. "Watch out for Edie," he said. "She's a pain in the ass and fights everything we do. She has wasted an easy million in taxpayer dollars with her zero-development philosophy." He was right. Edie perfectly fit that great Winston Churchill definition of an extremist: someone who will never change their mind and cannot change the subject.

Unfortunately, there was nothing we could do about it. The county had to respond to the suit. And according to local statute, the developer—that is, *us*—had to pay the county's legal costs for doing so.

What made the whole thing so painful was that I knew we would ultimately win the lawsuit. We'd done our homework, and the plans were all unassailably solid. The county really wanted the project. And since it had already been approved, the judge couldn't have outright killed it. At the very worst, he could have made us go back and do our environmental-impact reports over again. But the Sierra Club (that is, this one woman) wasn't backing down. If they (she) lost this suit, they (she) would just appeal it, which would have dragged it out for yet another long stretch of legal battles. It was a war of attrition, and since we were obligated to pay the county's legal bills, it was stacked in the plaintiff's favor.

There was no money left in our coffers. We had coasted over the finish line on fumes. It would take at least another half million to fight this thing. And with the economy in the shitter, nobody was about to step forward with the capital it would take to see it through.

By mid-2011 I had to acquiesce to the reality of the situation and call it quits.

I called the shareholders and let them know it was over. I had beaten Blackwater at their own game—and in return been beaten myself by a lady from the Sierra Club. It would have been funny if it weren't so crushing. I had dedicated five years of my life to this idea, bolstered with the majority of my modest net worth along with a ton of money from friends and family members—and it was all gone in the blink of a court filing.

Shortly after which, my wife asked me for a divorce.

As I said, life in the teams can be brutal on relationships. Despite my having left the service five years beforehand specifically in order to be at home more and strengthen my family life, it had been too late. My marriage had become another casualty of war.

And I had to admit, it wasn't just life as a SEAL. The fact was, I didn't know how to make a long-term relationship work. My own parents' marriage had become irretrievably fractured by the time I enlisted in the Navy. I thought I would be better at this than my dad, but now my own marriage hadn't lasted even past my oldest son's tenth birthday.

I had not succeeded in following in John's footsteps or honoring his example, in more ways than one. As dedicated as he was to his work, John was never the classic workaholic, sacrificing his family on the altar of his entrepreneurial dreams. I'd seen others do that. Not John. His business was always his driving passion, yet what he was most proud of and most in love with was his family, and he never let business get in the way.

But me? Here I was: savings blown; business dream up in smoke; marriage irrevocably on the rocks. Compared to this, the reign of Harvey had been a picnic. Because here, now, there was no Harvey to blame. Yes, there were villains in the picture, and I could point and say my plans had been sabotaged, both from without and within. But denial and evasion of responsibility are not part of a SEAL's makeup. I had to face the facts: I'd brought this all on myself.

It was the lowest point of my life.

After Wind Zero died, I had no idea how to pick up the pieces and go on. There were days when the idea of packing it all in, moving to Mexico, and living the simple life on my veteran's benefits sounded more tempting than I wanted it to. But I had kids here. There was no way I could walk away. Besides, giving up is something I'm just not wired to do.

And then there was John Zinn's example to honor.

Yes, I'd just experienced a massive failure. But John had tried dozens of ideas before Indigen Armor took off. If he could keep going, so could I.

Within a few months of tossing in the Wind Zero towel, I took a position as director at L-3 Communications, a large defense company in San Diego, just so I'd have something that paid the bills. It was a solid job and excellent money, but it drove me stir-crazy. I felt like a rat in a cage. I had to *do* something.

Ironically, it was that smear campaign against me and Wind Zero from a few years before that ultimately provided the answer. When that anti–Brandon Webb video appeared online, a friend told me that the only way to push it off the first page of search results was to get a lot more content about me onto the Internet. So I started doing whatever I could to produce material. In the process, I discovered that I liked to write.

A few years before Wind Zero closed I was invited to blog for a large website that served the military community. I'd been doing that now for two years, and I enjoyed it. At the same time, I saw quite a few ways the site itself could be improved. In fact, there was no single site that served the whole Special Operations community. So I decided to start my own. I invited a few friends from different branches of the service to write for the site as well. I scraped together about ten thousand dollars and launched SOFREP.com (for Special Operations Forces Situation Report) in January 2012.

By the end of the year we had more than a million people per month hitting our site.

All the success that had failed to materialize with Wind Zero happened with SOFREP. Within a year after launch I found myself running the largest Internet site in the world devoted to Special Operations. Our weekly SOFREP Radio podcast became the number one broadcast in its category (government) on iTunes, with more than half a million monthly visitors. The publishing division we launched had several *New York Times* bestsellers in its first year. Soon we had acquired or created more than half a dozen related websites, from NavySeals.com and the gear site Loadout Room to Fighter Sweep, a site dedicated to military and general aviation enthusiasts, and TransitionHQ, the only legitimate military-to-civilian advice and jobs portal on the Internet. We created an umbrella entity called Force12 Media to bring SOFREP and all the other properties together into one unified digital network. In just two years, Force12 Media went from a concept to a full-fledged digital-media empire.

I suppose I never did get out of the real estate business. I just shifted from developing one kind of site to another kind.

Through SOFREP and Force12 I've doubled the income I was earning at L-3 as a salaried employee, and done it working for myself, on my own terms. It's a lot of work, and it keeps me extremely busy.

But not so busy that it runs my life or makes me miserable. Over the past few years, even with the craziness of Force12, I've also made it my business to take the time to build an excellent relationship with my ex-wife and her family, and to be there, consistently and in a big way, for our children.

That was another lesson I learned from John Zinn. Maybe the most important one of all.

After all the struggle and heartache of Wind Zero, the success of Force12 Media has been a gratifying experience, to say the least. There is a bittersweet note to it, though. Because I would have so loved to share the story of it all with John. I owed him that. But he was no longer there to share it with.

In 2010, less than a year after selling his company, John was in Amman, Jordan, at a huge military equipment expo. He was out with a few SEAL buddies but decided to turn in early, as he had an appointment early the next day to demo his latest vehicle to the king of Jordan. On the way home, he had his cabdriver stop the car so he could get out and walk the rest of the way. He never made it back to his hotel.

Exactly what happened is shrouded in uncertainty. According to the cabdriver's testimony, John was agitated about something when he bolted from the cab and walked off on his own, headed for a rough section of town. It could just as well have been that the cabdriver was heading to the wrong hotel and that John, realizing this, got out of the cab and in typical John fashion decided to forge his own path. According to official reports, he stumbled on his walk home and fell off a steep drop in the path. According to the SEAL who saw him off in the cab that night, he was sober and clearheaded, and "stumbled on his walk home" just doesn't sound like John. One report ruled out foul play; another cited "suspicious circumstances."

The chances are good we'll never know every fact and detail about exactly what happened that night. What we do know is this: The world is not a safe place. And John died making it a lot safer.

John was not on active duty or in the thick of combat when he perished. But Glen Doherty was right, in his toast to Dave Scott in that little Filipino bar in October 2002, when he said, "We all signed up for this. It's all part of the deal." As we say when we join the Spec Ops world, we're writing a check, payable to the U.S. government, and in the "amount" section it says "up to and including our lives." John left behind two daughters, ages two and four, and Jackie was pregnant with their first son, Matthew, whom John was so looking forward to meeting. He was a good friend, one of the best, and was busy serving his country and his fellow warriors right to his last breath.

John was a visionary. He had the capacity to paint a picture that others found so compelling, so real, that they would follow and do whatever it took to support him and help bring that picture into reality. It's an ability, I've come to see, that every leader needs to master, whether you're leading a platoon of warriors in combat or a team of colleagues or employees in a business venture.

And he was a visionary in a larger sense, too, in that he saw the direction the world was headed and led the way. The wave of the future in our military presence is not in large masses of forces invading territories, but with small, highly adaptable units, like Spec Ops individuals. The ability to be discreet, to have a small footprint as you go into a country and quietly look around without being obvious, is pivotal to the tactical and strategic successes of the future. John's idea was ahead of its time. It still is.

5

ROUGH MEN
STANDING BY

CHRIS CAMPBELL, HEATH ROBINSON,
AND JT TUMILSON

On April 14, 2009, I drove into the heart of downtown San Diego to hunt down an address I'd been given via e-mail, a little hole-in-the-wall off Market Street. Inside, the guy running the place ushered me into a tiny room, where he sat me in a chair in front of a green-screen backdrop, facing a television camera. "This thing is piped directly into the studio in New York," he told me. *And right into a hundred million households*, I thought. *Hi, everyone, Brandon here.*

Earlier that day an e-mail had landed in my in-box asking whether I would be willing to be interviewed on live national television for CNN. It was just two days since an American sea captain had been rescued from pirates off the coast of Somalia by three simultaneous shots fired by three Navy SEAL snipers. Someone from Anderson Cooper's office had learned about me and my role in the NSW sniper course and tracked me down. Would I be willing to go on *Anderson Cooper 360°* that night to talk about these men and their training? Like, in a few hours?

Sure, I replied. So there I was.

This would be my first time appearing before the media in any major way, and I was a little nervous. People who do this all the time—celebrities, politicians, big business executives—typically go through media training and get extensive coaching to prepare for live TV. The only coaching I was going to get was this guy nodding in the direction of the lens.

He wired me with a nearly invisible earpiece and pointed out the monitor parked next to the camera. Christiane Amanpour's lips were moving, but there was no sound coming out. "Don't try to look at the person on the other end," he said. "It'll mess you up because of the time delay. Look right into the camera, or it'll look like you're being evasive." I nodded. Some good coaching after all. Then he left the room.

The place felt airless. I could reach out and touch the walls on both sides at the same time. Suddenly Christiane Amanpour's voice was in my head.

". . . It was marksmanship at its best—the way Brandon Webb teaches it"—it sounded like she was sitting directly next to me, her mouth to my ear—"and he joins us now from San Diego. Brandon, I think everybody wants to know how three coordinated shots, different people shooting at a moving target from a moving platform, just how did they do it? And how difficult was it?"

I talked for the next two or three minutes, doing my best to answer Amanpour's questions. But I knew the question all her viewers were really asking:

Who are *these guys—and how the hell do they do what they do?*

I'll tell you who they are: some of the best, kindest, noblest men I've ever known.

. . .

The Captain Phillips rescue generated an enormous swell of interest among the public. And with good reason. By the spring of 2009, America was tired of failing. Wall Street had just self-destructed, the housing market had crashed, and the economy was going down in flames. War in the Middle East was dragging on with no end in sight. The rest of the world community was looking at us like we were the kid who stank up the whole room by shitting our pants and were too clueless to realize it. We couldn't seem to do *anything* right. The nation was hungry for heroes.

Three months earlier, on a crisp January day, a US Airways pilot named Chesley Sullenberger had saved a passenger plane from crashing into the Hudson by flying it like a glider. Sullenberger's performance had a seismic impact on the national morale. It was like a sign from above that maybe our country *was* still capable of producing someone who could pull off a classic American can-do miracle.

And now these three anonymous SEAL snipers had pulled off a stunt so perfect you'd think it was lifted out of a James Bond film.

The Captain Phillips rescue faded eventually from the news cycle, but the current of public interest in the SEAL community continued surging along. Two years later it burst onto the front pages again, this time in an even bigger wave than before. On the evening of May 1, 2011, President Obama interrupted Donald Trump's *Celebrity Apprentice* to stride up to a White House podium and make the announcement that we'd just completed a successful raid on a suburban complex in Pakistan and killed America's public enemy number one.

It's impossible to overstate the impact and sense of historical vindication the UBL (bin Laden) raid's success ignited in our nation. It wasn't just the ghost of September 11 being avenged at last. The feeling of payback and resolution reached decades farther back, all the way to the original formation of U.S. Special Operations Command (SOCOM).

I was only five years old when President Jimmy Carter sent a contingent of Spec Ops troops into Iran in a failed attempt to rescue the American hostages, but the reverberations of that disaster were still echoing well into the new century. Operation Eagle Claw, as it was called, ended catastrophically, leaving one helo crashed and five abandoned, eight servicemen dead, our fifty-two hostages still captive, and America thoroughly humiliated. It was a classic right-hand-doesn't-know-what-the-left-hand's-doing fuckup. And it was in direct response to that colossal failure that SOCOM was created—a unified structure bringing together the Spec Ops forces of the different branches under one centralized command. The bin Laden raid not only nailed the architect of the 9/11 attacks; it also presented the ultimate demonstration that we'd learned from that thirty-year-old debacle and gotten our shit wired tight.

To Eagle Claw's lingering question mark, Neptune Spear was one hell of an exclamation point.

The moment news of the UBL raid hit the media, the world went crazy over the highly secretive—and up till this point highly secret—Spec Ops unit involved, and that same question was once again on everyone's lips: *Who the hell* are *these guys?*

First, let me tell you who they're not.

They're not Disney action figures. And they're not the macho muscle guys you typically see acted out on the big screen. When the film *Zero Dark Thirty* came out, most of us in Spec Ops could barely watch it. Yes, it was that bad. That final scene, when the SEALs are taking the bin Laden compound and the whole team runs around the building, sweeping one another with their lasers, and then they barge in doing that ridiculous movie-assault-team shout, "Go, go, go, go, *go!*"—it was fucking painful. No excuse, Hollywood, no excuse.

No, in real life these men are not steroidal supermen or one-dimensional fighting freaks. They are ordinary flesh-and-blood human beings who shape-shift themselves into something extraordinary through sheer will and devotion.

Like three of my friends, Chris, Heath, and JT.

I met Chris Campbell when he rolled into my BUD/S class in 1997. Chris was living proof that you cannot judge a book by its cover. He stood about five-seven, one of the smallest guys in our class, and weighed maybe 140 sopping wet. The instructors called him "Campbell's Soup," because he always had a smile on his face, like the happy cartoon kid on the soup can. No matter how much shit they threw at him, it wouldn't stick. Chris was afraid of nothing, never lost his temper, and nothing could faze him. You just could not get this guy down.

One night during second phase (this was after making it through Hell Week in first phase), we were winding down for the night when one of our instructors screeched into the parking lot, braked his car on a crazy angle, and got out, leaving his headlights on. We heard him outside telling the other instructors, "Go home, you guys. I've got this." Instructor Weber, as we could clearly hear from his slurred speech, was piss-drunk. He was going through a divorce at the time, and he was not a happy man. What was more, he was prepared to share that state generously with the rest of us.

Instructor Weber walked into the building and started laying into the class, yelling at us, hosing us down, and subjecting us to various forms of punishment. As he stood regarding the group, his head swiveling slowly left to right like a tank gun, his eyes lit on me. I didn't know what was going on behind those reddened eyes, but whatever it was, it wasn't good.

"Hey, Webb," he growled. "So you got time to go grab a dry shirt? *Fuck you.*" That was when I knew I was in for some trouble.

Somehow Instructor Weber knew I'd had a dry T-shirt on earlier that night. In fact, when we suited up in our wet suits to go out into the surf, I never wore a T-shirt underneath like everyone else did. (I never understood this. I mean, why bother? It just gets wet!) I'd do my dive, take my wet suit off, put my dry T-shirt on, and then everyone would be standing around in wet T-shirts except me. This little luxury I allowed myself had just come back to bite me in the ass.

Nearby stood a large tank of clean, freezing-cold water that we'd use to wash the sand and salt water off our gear and regulators after being in the ocean—the dip tank. Weber glared at me emptily, then swiveled his tank-gun gaze over and looked at Chris. Then over at the dip tank. Then back at us. I could see the words forming in his brain before he hacked them up and coughed them at us.

"Webb! Campbell! In the dip tank!"

Whatever infraction Chris had committed that earned his being in there with me, I don't remember or never knew in the first place. But there we were, up to our necks in freezing-cold water, watching the rest of the class doing push-ups and eight-count bodybuilders while Weber talked. And talked. The guy went on and on: what shits we were, how miserable this class was, how we'd never make it to third phase, what an embarrassment we presented. Soon he was getting circular. *Oh, God*, I thought, *when is this going to be over?* I was positive that death from hypothermia was only minutes away. I couldn't imagine being more miserable. I felt so sorry for myself.

And then I glanced over at Campbell.

His teeth were chattering so hard they sounded like they were going to rattle right out of his head—*rat-tat-tat-tat-tat-tat-tat*, like a chipmunk machine gun. And he had this big shit-eating grin on his face. I did a literal double take and wondered whether I was hallucinating. What the hell would he have to be so happy about? Yet there it was, that classic Campbell grin plastered on his mug—and so help me, *I was grinning back*.

It occurred to me then how ridiculous we both looked. And how inane Instructor Weber's endless rant sounded. And how absurd the whole situation was. And then Chris and I were both laughing—at our own misery and everything about it.

That moment was perfect Campbell. And he had that effect on everyone. No matter what was going on, no matter how bad the situation got, things always seemed easier when Chris was around. Everyone liked him. How could you *not*?

I heard a story about Chris from Randy Kelley (the same Randy Kelley who later helped me out when I was launching the Wind Zero effort). Randy and Chris were teammates in the BUD/S class before mine, before Chris got rolled. During

Hell Week there's an exercise we call Around the World, where you go out onto the ocean in the middle of the night and paddle around Coronado Island. This is essentially an endurance contest, an all-night affair that runs from the early evening through dawn the next day. On this occasion it was deep in the middle of the night, they'd been out there paddling in the frigid Pacific for hours, and everyone was starting to pass out from the cold and lack of sleep. Randy had grown up going to a Baptist church, and at that moment the tune of an old Baptist hymn popped into his mind. Desperate to keep himself awake, he started humming it.

Suddenly Randy heard another voice harmonizing with his. Chris had joined in, and not only that, he was singing the words. Randy looked over at Chris. They both laughed, then started in again, singing this old hymn together. The other guys on the boat groaned and said, "Jesus, you guys." Which only made them laugh harder—and keep on singing.

It turned out Chris and Randy had both grown up in North Carolina. They hit it off and stuck together from that point on, even after Chris rolled out of that BUD/S class and into the next. After BUD/S they both went on to Team Five and ended up in the same platoon, where they became inseparable.

Chris had joined the SEALs in large part because he wanted to get out of North Carolina and see the world. He and Randy both loved the outdoors, and whenever the platoon arrived at a new location, if it was possible to camp out, they would take that option over a hotel room. While the other guys would go out partying, Chris and Randy would go exploring—on safari, diving, hiking, whatever. For the next four years, through two platoons, they did this all around the world.

A devoted photographer, Chris always had a camera with him, taking pictures of anything and everything. The others would ride him for what seemed like stupid things to snap pictures of at the time. But when they'd get back home and look at the photos he'd taken, they would turn out to be amazing shots. The dude had an eye; that was for sure. In fact, the thing Randy noticed most about Campbell was his capacity to appreciate the beauty of whatever was going on, to be at home wherever he was. No matter where *here* was at the moment, he never seemed to want to be anywhere else.

"What's special about Chris," said Randy, "is not that he's larger-than-life. It's kind of like he *is* life."

Chris's progress through SEAL training was not an easy time for him. In fact, in those early years it almost seemed like he had to work extra hard just to keep up.

Near the end of third phase in BUD/S, we were doing a final land-navigation exercise up at Camp Pendleton. Land nav was tough. We were out in the mountains through the freezing nights, snow on the ground. We didn't get much sleep. Most of land nav we went through in groups, but this final exercise dissolved the squads. Now it was every man for himself. The air crackled with tension. We all knew that if we didn't pass, we didn't graduate.

The exercise was a combination of survival skills and navigation/reconnaissance skills. The instructors had planted a series of navigation points distributed across the country-side, spanning a number of mountains. We had to hit each point in the right sequence, almost like a survivalist scavenger hunt. At each point there was an ammo box with a unique code inside that we had to radio in along with our coordinates before moving on to the next.

In the middle of the night, I ran into Chris. He looked disheveled and frazzled.

"Hey, man," I said, "what's going on?"

He jerked his head in my direction and stared at me. "I just realized, this isn't my point! I'm not supposed to be on *this* hill!" He pointed to a mountain about two miles away. "I'm supposed to be on *that* hill!" And he went staggering off in the other direction.

Oh, man, I thought. *Campbell is fucked.* And he almost was. He nearly flunked out of BUD/S on that land nav. The next morning I checked in with him to see how he'd done. He'd made all his points, all right, but in the process he'd gotten a severe case of poison oak. The poor guy was covered with it. Anyone else would have been in utter misery. Not Campbell. There he was, lying on a rolled-out mat on the ground, covered head to toe with that ugly red, burning rash, grinning and laughing at some joke.

If you'd been a betting man and you were around when Chris was going through those early years of training, your money probably would not have been on his being the guy who would go on to become an outstanding operator. His spirit was Teflon, but this SEAL stuff did not come easy for him.

Not long after 9/11, Chris and Randy's platoon went into a given location in the Middle East to assess possible access points, in case it proved impossible to airdrop forces directly into landlocked Afghanistan. Randy was the platoon's leading petty officer, so it was his responsibility to make sure everyone had all the right gear. After they finished their surveys and were preparing to pull out, Chris approached him on the beach. "Hey, Randy," he said. "I, well . . . I lost my gun."

"No way," Randy said. That wasn't possible. For a SEAL, there are few infractions as catastrophic as losing your gun. We would always, *always* have our sidearms strapped in, and we would always, *always* lanyard our guns, especially when we were going in the ocean.

Chris showed Randy his holster. No gun.

"Tell me you lost it somewhere here, right?" said Randy, gesturing up and down the stretch of beach.

Chris hung his head. "No, man. It's nowhere on the beach. It's gotta be in the ocean somewhere."

Even aside from being a SEAL, Chris was an avid outdoorsman who had always loved the ocean. He would spend hours surfing the waves. The ocean was like his home. This was the last guy in the world you'd think would be unprepared for an op in the water. But the gun was gone.

There was nothing Randy could do to help Chris out here. As LPO he had to tell the platoon commander. He did. The commander went ballistic.

They spent the next six hours diving in the surf, trying to find that gun, until the sun went down and the boats came in to take them back to their ship.

Chris was on kitchen duty on the ship for the next two weeks. That may sound like light punishment, but let me explain something: SEALs are *never* on kitchen duty. It just doesn't happen. There may be several hundred crew members, sailors, Marines, and others on a ship—and a few dozen SEALs, who are regarded as being in a class by themselves. I've seen high-ranking officers step aside and let a teams guy through when they see that trident. Kitchen duty? You must be kidding. It was unspeakably humiliating for Chris.

It also became a defining moment for his career. He felt he'd let everyone down—and it drove him to double his effort to become an outstanding performer. Which was exactly what he did. Not long after the lost-gun episode, Chris went on to Green Team, which is to top-tier operations what BUD/S is to the SEALs. It is one ballbusting tryout, and more than half who start don't make it through.

Including Chris. He failed out of Green Team.

And then something amazing happened: They kept him around.

It's hard to convey just how rare this is. When you fail out of Green Team, you fail out—emphasis on the word *out*. In that way Green Team is *not* like BUD/S: You don't get a second try. And you don't stick around, either; you are sent back to your regular SEAL team, where you resume your career. You do not pass Go or move around the board again. Incredibly, though, they let Chris stay. His instructors gave him a temporary billet somewhere at their command, doing boring administrative and support tasks. Basically, being a whipping boy. But still: They let him stay.

Why? Because of that Chris Campbell attitude. They could see he was dead serious and very conscientious and at the same time completely humble, both about himself and his job. They couldn't help it; they just *liked* him.

And he worked his ass off. After about a year of this he went back through Green Team a second time. This time he made it. As an outstanding operator, he became part of incredibly exacting and dangerous missions that you and I have never read about in the papers or heard about on CNN, and never will.

And then there was Heath Robinson.

In the summer of 2001, long after Chris Campbell had joined Team Five and I'd gone to Team Three, after going through sniper school and deployment and the USS *Cole* and home again, I left my friends at Golf Platoon to help resurrect a struggling Echo Platoon that was going through a major restructuring. It had a new chief, Chris Dye, who was excellent, and a small handful of solid, squared-away guys who made my job a hell of a lot easier than it might have been. Heath Robinson was one of them.

The first day I met Heath, I had just hopped a C-2 Greyhound COD (carrier on-board delivery) monoplane to meet up with Echo a few hundred miles off the San Diego coast, where they were stationed on an aircraft carrier in the Pacific preparing for some GOPLATs (gas and oil platform) boarding work. The next morning I started jocking up with them for a ship-boarding exercise where we'd be fast-roping down from two helos. Right away I saw we were in trouble. These guys had their shit dangling all over the place.

Even with the intense level of training we get in the SEALs, there's still a substantial chasm between the learning you do in the classroom and the learning you get from real-world experience. These guys didn't know how to tighten up their straps, cut off the excess, and tape things down where necessary. They had no idea how to position or sling their guns properly. They were so *not* ready for serious action it wasn't funny. It made me realize how much I'd taken our leadership at Golf Platoon for granted. Later that day, while we were on the exercise, one dude (a train wreck of a guy whom we eventually had to shit-can during our Afghanistan deployment) actually dropped his rifle in the middle of a maneuver on one of the helos—an unpardonable sin. Their chief didn't see it. I did.

After the exercise the chief took us through a debriefing, then asked if I had any comments. I let loose, giving them chapter and verse on just how fucked-up and unprepared they were.

Later on that day one of the team, a guy with intense eyes set in a Hollywood-handsome face, came over to talk to me. "Petty Officer Webb?" he said.

"Yeah," I said.

"I just want to thank you for joining our platoon."

"No problem," I told him. "Glad to help."

"Also," he added, "can you take a few minutes to show me what the hell I'm doing?"

Right then and there I got all I ever needed to know about Heath Robinson: He was fanatical about learning and doing whatever it took to become the best operator possible; he was both outgoing and disarmingly self-deprecating; and he was fucking hilarious. His smile lit up every room he entered.

While he was going through BUD/S, one night Heath and his fellow inmates were lying wet and sandy in the surf, arms linked in a chain of suffering. Where Campbell and Kelley had sung a Baptist hymn to keep their spirits up, Heath went a different way. Suddenly his voice blurted out, "Flintstones, *meet* the Flintstones . . ." and everyone in the class burst out laughing.

That was Heath to a T: entertaining, colorful, funny as hell. His sense of humor and perfectly timed one-liners got a lot of guys through those long, dark nights of the soul.

Heath was a born ham and loved to perform. In grade school he played Scrooge in a school production of Charles Dickens's *A Christmas Carol*, and had a blast doing it. Get a few beers in him and he could do a pitch-perfect rendition of Michael Jackson's "Thriller." The other guys called him Hollywood, in part because he was such a good-looking guy and a classy dresser, and in part because he loved the movies and was constantly cracking people up with well-placed film lines. In the fall of 2001, as we were about to put down on a blood-soaked tarmac in war-torn Kandahar in the wake of a Marine invasion: "Six bucks and my right nut say we're not landing in Chicago" (*Planes, Trains and Automobiles*). As we were listening to a teammate grunt in pain while being stitched up in the field by an impatient corpsman: "I'll have what she's having" (*When Harry Met Sally*). As we were about to embark on a mission tracking down Taliban forces on the Afghanistan-Pakistan border just before dawn: "Use of unnecessary violence in the apprehension of the Blues Brothers *has* been approved" (*The Blues Brothers*). It sure made everyday life easier over there. Heath's saxophone traveled with him through Afghanistan, too. In later deployments his priorities shifted, and the sax was replaced by what came to be known as Heath's Famous Cappuccino Machine.

Heath grew up in Petoskey, on the northern tip of Michigan. Like Matt Axelson, Heath had the Navy in his blood. His grandfather on his mother's side served in World War II in the Navy, and he and Heath were very close throughout Heath's childhood and beyond.

Heath told me that when he was sixteen, he watched on CNN as the bodies of American servicemen were dragged through the streets of Mogadishu while the American flag burned. "That was the moment I knew I wanted to become a Navy SEAL," he said. "I wanted to stop things like that from happening."

I took him under my wing and we quickly became friends. Up to that point the guys in Echo had had no real leadership. With the platoon's reorganization, Chief Dye, my BUD/S teammate Shawn, a few other more experienced guys coming on board, and I managed to quickly bring the platoon up to snuff, but only through serious browbeating and 'round-the-clock abuse. Heath ate it up. Despite being a new guy he soon proved a more valuable asset to the team than some of the more experienced SEALs in the platoon. He was not even two years out of BUD/S, but he was so determined to become a first-rate SEAL, and so hungry to do things right, that by the time we were in Afghanistan, being with him felt like being with a seasoned operator.

Heath's work ethic became legendary in the teams. There's another story about him in BUD/S. It was second phase, which is focused on swimming, and the guys were getting their pool certification, which is a pretty brutal process. Heath was a compact guy, maybe five-eight, built like a wrestler (he wrestled in high school), but the water was not his native element, as it was for those of us who grew up on the coast, like John Zinn or Chris Campbell. He was not doing well. After three attempts, he still had not passed. The pool instructor yelled, "Robinson! Get out; you're finished!" then yanked him out of the pool and started berating him. Heath stood there listening intently, taking it all in. As soon as the instructor turned his back, assuming that Heath would go ring out and leave, defeated, Heath instead jumped back in the pool.

"You see that?" screamed another instructor. *"That's what we're looking for!"* That night, Heath passed the pool-cert test.

When we were in Afghanistan together in 2001, Heath started talking about going on to a top-tier unit. That was his plan right from the start. After we came back home in the spring of 2002, he went over to Team Seven, where he did one more platoon. Two years after that he was off to nine months of advanced training and then right into that top-tier unit, where he proceeded to rack up a long list of medals and decorations, including four Bronze Star medals, three of them with the coveted V for Valor and one for extraordinary heroism.

Here's how that last one happened.

In February 2011, Heath was part of a mission involving East African pirates who had kidnapped and then killed a number of civilian hostages.

After the team silently boarded the ship, the lead guy slipped into a seemingly empty cabin. It was tight quarters and piss-poor lighting—and, as it turned out, not empty after all: One of the pirates was crouching hidden in the darkest recess. The SEAL entered slowly. The room remained silent for the span of a second or two. Then the pirate leaped out and jumped him from behind, yanking him off his feet. Heath was the number two guy through the door and instantly saw what was happening, but he couldn't engage with his primary (rifle) or his secondary (sidearm) without risking injury to his buddy.

Long gone were those painful early days of Echo Platoon and its new guys who had no clue how to sling their weapons. Heath had burned his training into his bones. Reacting faster than the speed of thought, he slung his M4, and in one smooth motion his custom Dan Winkler knife was out and slashing across the man's throat. Swift as a shark attack and just as deadly. Seconds later the pirate was on the floor without heartbeat or brain wave, and Heath's teammate was free and very much alive. I know, I know: You've seen moves like this happen in action flicks. But you have to remember: That's the world of fantasy and make-believe. In real life it's a split-second complex of exacting maneuvers that can go wrong in a thousand ways, and often do. Heath's flawless execution saved his teammate's life and left Heath with one of the few certified knife kills on record since Vietnam. (Heath's mom still has that knife.)

Heath had no tolerance for shoddiness, and he became famous in the teams for how intense he got when straightening out a sloppy performance. He could go from calm to raging in seconds, his face reddening and looking like he was about to burst a vessel. His teammates dubbed it "the Heath Stroke." There are quite a few guys out there who are alive today because they were subjected to the Heath Stroke when lives were *not* on the line, and who became better operators as a result.

When Heath made chief in 2007, he phoned home to give his mom the news. "Tell Grandpa for me. He's the only one in the family who will understand what that really means."

Three years later Heath went one better and made senior chief.

Heath would sign his e-mails with this quote, attributed to George Orwell:

We sleep peacefully in our beds because rough men stand
by to visit violence on those that would do us harm.

It was more than just a sig line. As sensitive, amiable, and funny a guy as he was, he was more than willing to be one of those rough men when circumstances demanded it. Heath brought more peaceful sleep to our shores than many of us will ever know.

The third of these three friends of mine was a sniper student who came through our course in 2005, long after Matt Axelson and the Luttrell brothers had graduated. His name was Jon Tumilson. JT, we called him.

My first conversation with JT happened in my office, which by this time was not underground in the Coronado bunker but in an aboveground building in another location. I had called JT in to let him know that I wanted him to be the class leader for that session. The two reasons I remember this so clearly are that I could immediately see 1) how perfectly suited to the job he was, and 2) how uncomfortable this made him.

Class leader was no mere honorary or symbolic title. In the NSW sniper course, the class leader has his work cut out for him. Keeping a pack of alpha-male Navy SEALs in line for three solid months of long, punishing days is not a job for the faint of heart. I would meet with the class leader every day, brief him on what the next day's evolution was and what it would involve, explain where I wanted him and the rest of the class to be, and go over the schedule. It was his job to make sure the class was prepared and squared away. If they weren't, it was to some extent his ass that would be on the line.

Just as I had with Matt Axelson and JT's BUD/S teammate Morgan Luttrell (and later with Marcus), I took JT as one of my personal students and spent time mentoring him every day throughout that session. He turned out to be the best damn class leader I ever had. His reluctance notwithstanding, JT knew how to drop the hammer. He rarely needed to do it, though. Nobody gave him any trouble during those three months. They respected him too much.

JT was a quiet, tall Iowa boy, six-foot-five, with an economical frame, dark hair, hazel green eyes, and a gentle, easygoing personality, hugely popular throughout his school years. A friend once described him as a "human Labrador: smart, athletic, and you want him to be with you everywhere you go"—an inside joke, as JT's one constant companion was his chocolate Lab, Hawkeye. JT was devoted to his family, driving home to see them every chance he could. One December he called home to say he couldn't make it for Christmas that year. When Christmas came JT's sister Joy (who was in on the secret) led the family outside to find a huge present sitting there, a wrapped box as big as a three-drawer filing cabinet. They tore the wrapping paper off the top and looked inside—and there was JT, sitting cross-legged and grinning up at them.

Lurking underneath that easygoing personality was a ferociously disciplined athlete. JT was a wrestler throughout his school years, competed in marathons and triathlons, and was a dedicated and accomplished distance runner.

When JT was a kid he had no interest in reading. As far as he was concerned, if the teacher couldn't put it in words right there in the class, why should he have to spend his time sitting in a chair, extracting it from a book? He'd much rather be outside running, jumping, or climbing. Or in the gym wrestling. His mother told him she would buy him any book he wanted, on any topic ("as long as it isn't smut"), if he would agree to read it. Toward the end of his freshman year of high school, when JT was fifteen, he asked for a copy of a book that had just been published: *Rogue Warrior*, Richard Marcinko's wilder-than-fiction memoir. A controversial SEAL with combat roots in the Vietnam War, Marcinko was the first commander of that top-tier unit decades ago. *Rogue Warrior* was strong stuff, and JT ate it up, loved every word of it. The moment he put that book down, he was on a mission, reading everything he could dig up on the SEALs (which was damned hard to find in those pre-Internet days). From that point on, every book report and class project was about the SEALs. He knew more about the teams as a fifteen- and sixteen-year-old than most frogmen know when they first sign up for BUD/S.

JT enlisted in the summer of '94, following his junior year of high school, with plans to jump into boot camp a year later, immediately after graduation, and make a beeline for BUD/S. Not so fast, they told him: The SEAL pipeline was full at the moment. Instead they suggested he go into intelligence, which could serve as a stepping-stone to BUD/S. When he finished A school at the top of his class, they gave him his pick of assignments. For a boy from a tiny Iowa town (Rockford: population 850), Hawaii sounded pretty appealing. Hawaii it was; he got orders to the state-of-the-art guided-missile cruiser USS *Port Royal*, which had just been commissioned.

JT loved his time in Hawaii and was enormously popular, both with his teammates and with the local female population. One year he posed shirtless for a "Men of Hawaii" calendar. (He was Mr. February.) The other guys teased him unmercifully and said he could make good money modeling, and thus his nickname was born: JT Money. As with Heath Robinson and "Hollywood," the name had more than one meaning: JT also had a reputation for spending money on wining and dining the ladies. There's no other way to say it: Women just loved JT. He was the ultimate ladies' man. Unlike the stereotypical bad-boy heartbreaker, though, he left no trail of resentment or ill will behind him. All the women who loved JT had nothing but good things to say about him, even after he broke up with them. They all understood that his first love would always be the teams.

That had been a given since he'd picked up his now dog-eared—and, eventually, personally autographed by the author—copy of *Rogue Warrior*.

After six full years in the regular fleet Navy, JT finally made it to BUD/S in October 2001, starting just weeks after the planes crashed into the towers, making his career as a SEAL precisely contemporaneous with the new era of warfare that came to be known as the Global War on Terrorism. He finished Class 238 in April 2002, and did his workup as the initial Afghanistan operation was winding down and the invasion of Iraq was winding up. He went on to do two deployments in Iraq, earning a Bronze Star for bravery during a firefight in one of them, and two in Afghanistan before joining Green Team.

What made JT such a great class leader was not simply his own excellence as an operator. While unquestionable, that alone would not have been sufficient; I've known plenty of impressive shooters who could never have exercised the leadership he did. It was his empathy and gift for bringing people together. The dude was so clearly wired as a social animal. At a wrestling match when he was just seven, a coach told his parents, "Jon may or may not win this match, but I can tell you this: Before it's over he's going to know how many brothers and sisters that other kid has and what he ate for breakfast." JT went to a lot of high school graduation parties for guys on the opposing teams. JT used to keep extra keys to all his friends' apartments. If another guy was out on deployment and JT was back home, he would go over and play with the kids, fix a broken dishwasher, do whatever needed doing to keep the home front solid and happy.

When JT first left home to join the Navy and make his way toward becoming part of the teams, one of his mother's friends said to her, "I just hope they don't take his sensitivity away from him."

We didn't.

And that's the point I most want to convey about JT, and about Heath, and about Chris Campbell: All three of them had such kind, generous natures. "Sensitive" may not be a word you expect in a description of the nation's deadliest war fighters. But there it is.

So: *Who are* these guys?

As I said, they are not your typical Hollywood pumped-up gladiators. They don't serve as the "rough men" of Heath's e-mail sig line because it's in their intrinsic nature to be rough. They *make* it their nature. They do this out of love and the undeniable drive to keep the rest of us safe.

Back in April 2009, as I sat in my claustrophobic booth in downtown San Diego waiting for Christiane Amanpour's voice to come over my earpiece, I didn't know exactly who had been on that mission to rescue Captain Phillips, but the three men I thought about were Campbell, Heath, and JT. I thought about what solid guys and thoughtful friends they were, how devoted they were to their families, what grueling training they'd gone through and insane odds they had overcome to become the warriors they were, and how much service they had given to so many of us sleeping peacefully in our beds, we who would never know more than a fraction of all that they did to protect us.

I thought of them again two years later in 2011, when I heard about the UBL raid, although none of these three was on that particular mission.

And then I thought of them again three months after that.

On August 6, 2011, a Chinook-47 transport helicopter, call sign Extortion 17, on its way to support a nighttime raid in the Tangi Valley west of Kabul, was shot down by three RPGs fired by Taliban forces, killing all thirty-eight on board, including seventeen SEALs, five Navy Spec Ops support personnel, five Army aircrew, and three Air Force ground support personnel, as well as seven Afghan commandos, one Afghan interpreter, and one U.S. military dog. It was the single largest loss of American lives in our ten years of war in Afghanistan.

I heard the news about the same time everyone else did. All we knew at first was that seventeen SEALs had died in the crash, along with more than twenty others. When I heard the numbers I murmured to myself, "Oh, man . . . there were people I know on that helo." Sure enough, there were.

Campbell was on board.

So was Heath.

And JT.

Have you ever taken a punch square in the solar plexus, right below the sternum? If you have, then you know what happens next. Your diaphragm contracts to the size of a mung bean; you feel like throwing up and passing out at the same time and are horrified to realize that you don't have the strength to do either one. You can't breathe, you can't move, and you can't think. You don't just collapse; you implode. You feel like you've been turned into a sock puppet, with no will or agency of your own, and it would be funny if you weren't in agony, which you are, times one hundred.

If you've ever had that experience, then you have a sense of how it felt to read the list of names from the Extortion 17 crash.

A teammate from my BUD/S days. A close friend from those touch-and-go days in the caves of Afghanistan. And one of our finest student leaders from the sniper course. Training; deployment; teaching. All three chapters of my SEAL career were on that helo.

It felt like my *life* had been shot down there in the Hindu Kush.

When you read casualty figures, you obviously know you're reading about a tragedy. What the numbers don't convey and few really grasp is the full impact an event like this has on our military. These men are not resources you can simply replace. You don't train a Spec Ops warrior in a few months, or even a few years. In strategic terms, the loss to the Spec Ops community was crippling. "It's like an entire NFL football team wiped out," said one Spec Ops officer at the time. "Like the department of surgery at Cornell medical school [gone]."

For me, it was the loss of too many friends. I know men in their eighties who are at the point in life when they are starting to lose their friends. You expect this to happen when you reach your eighties. You do not expect it in your thirties.

A friend of mine was in charge of the CACO (Casualty Assistance Calls Officer) effort. He had an entire department under him, some forty guys, tasked with all kinds of things people don't normally think about that are involved when something like this happens. For example, they had to pore over all the personal effects left behind by those who'd been killed. And, of course, they had to drive up to all those addresses, walk up to all those doors, and notify all those family members—wives, parents, children—that their husbands, their sons, their fathers were gone. Were not returning.

"It got really personal," said my friend. When I asked him to describe the experience, he had just two words: "A nightmare." He thought for a moment, then added, "That was the hardest thing I've ever done." And trust me: This is a guy who has done some hard things.

JT's coffin was flown out to his hometown in Iowa to a small airport in nearby Mason City, about a half hour away. The motorcade bringing JT to Rockford, led by hundreds of Patriot Guard Riders on motorcycles, drew people from far and wide. At one point Kathy Tumilson, JT's mother, saw a semi parked off the road on the other side of the interstate, driver standing at attention by his inert rig, hat over his heart, as they drove by. People started showing up on the overpasses as the motorcade passed underneath, paying their respects. The closer they got to Rockford, the more people lined the overpasses. By the time they turned onto the blacktop to head into Rockford it was like a parade, people standing two and three deep, with posters and flags, many of them weeping. More than fifteen hundred people attended JT's funeral service—a number, it should be noted, that is nearly twice the entire population of Rockford.

At one point during the service, a friend led Hawkeye, JT's faithful chocolate Lab, silently up to the front of the gymnasium where the military casket sat draped with its American flag. Hawkeye lay down on the cold floor next to the casket and didn't move from that spot as the service continued. You might remember seeing that photo; within days it went viral, showing up in newspapers and on websites everywhere, the wordless expression of an intensely personal grief that resonated nationally.

At the time of the crash, Heath Robinson's grandfather had been ill for months. When he heard the news that his first grandson had died, it was too much. He died four days later, on August 10. "I have to go," he told his wife.

I think I understood how he felt. I think all of us in the teams understood how he felt.

. . .

There's been some controversy around the downing of Extortion 17, in part because there were such a large number of SEALs aboard this one helicopter. Most of that controversy is manufactured and groundless, spurred on by shameless partisan politics and base motivations. But there was one thing about it that has plagued me.

The SEALs who saw that helo shot down back in June 2005 said it was *not* an RPG but something much more powerful, a MANPAD (man-portable air defense missile) of some sort, that took the bird down. According to Peter Nealen, a former recon Marine sniper and veteran of Iraq and Afghanistan, "Had a suspected MANPAD been reported and verified, it's likely that loss of life in-theater linked to shot-down helicopters could have been prevented, including the controversial Extortion 17 crash that would happen years later" (*Operation Red Wings*, New York: St. Martin's Press, 2013).

Why *didn't* they include this crucial point in the after-action report on Operation Red Wings?

It's always risky to speculate, and since I was not privy to any part of that process when it occurred, speculation is all this is. But I would guess it was because they knew that if they did include it, they would create one hell of a shit storm that could seriously disrupt the way we were managing our air operations in that AO at the time. An RPG has no guidance system. A MANPAD, which is not a grenade but a type of missile, does. If we'd known we were potentially up against portable, shoulder-fired guided missiles in that theater, would we have been forced to upgrade the defensive

One of my most treasured photos: our Naval Special Warfare Sniper School's graduating class, June 12, 2000. That's Mike Bearden standing tall in the back row, second from left. My best friend, Glen Doherty, stands smack in the middle (of course). I'm squatting right in front of him, with the dark glasses.

For the last quarter of 1999, Mike Bearden was named "Junior Sailor of the Quarter," a top-honors award given to the "best of the best" of all sailors on their given ship, for "superior performance, outstanding achievements, exemplary personal conduct and military bearing, and demonstrated initiative in performance." (The "junior" refers to the award given to ranks E4 and below.)

Here's Mike after crushing an over-the-beach exercise, giving his teammate some encouraging words as usual. The other guy looks pretty beat-up by the training; Mike *never* looked beat-up, no matter how tough the exercise.

At age eight Mike was still small for his age—but always ready to get in the game.

Mike and Derenda's son, Holden, was just ten months old at the time of Mike's accident. Today he is a strapping big guy with an outsize personality just like his dad's.

Courtesy of Kathleen Colvert

Dave Scott first joined SEAL Team Four as an enlisted man in the early nineties, years before he joined our platoon at SEAL Team Three as an officer.

Courtesy of Kathleen Colvert

For Dave, leaping out the door of a C-130 at ten thousand feet was like stepping out for a stroll.

Dave, the impeccable perfectionist, on a workup with his Team Three platoon in 2002, shortly before his last deployment.

Dave was as ready for action at age twelve, in his wetsuit, as he would be as an adult. I think he was *born* ready for action.

Dave and Kat beaming with happiness on their first wedding anniversary, in June 2002, four months before Dave's fatal accident in the Pacific.

Top left: Matt Axelson (*on the right, here age three and a half*) and his big brother, Jeff (*age six*), were incredibly close.

Top right: Matt in the fall of '85, at the age of ten. His natural blond Afro used to drive him crazy; sometimes he'd sneak the family's dog clippers and buzz his own hair short.

Bottom right: Matt and his beautiful wife, Cindy, at their wedding. If you look close, you can see their eyes are both still teared up. That was one seriously happy day.

Top: This is one of my favorite photos of Matt; even in a cap and dark glasses, his quiet personality shines.

Right: Matt was always the total professional. Here he is in the field, in Afghanistan 2005, not long before Operation Red Wings, completely at ease and ready for anything.

As John Zinn's dad says, "John was hell on the M60," a machine gun he used with great skill.

John was an outstanding athlete and a competitive water polo player, so at home in the water his instructors nicknamed him Neptune. He was also the ultimate cool lifeguard in high school.

John, his wife, Jackie, and their two girls took time off at Lake Tahoe for Christmas in 2009, never imagining it would be their last Christmas together.

As passionate an entrepreneur as he was, John was never a workaholic. His family always came first, and taking time to chill with his two girls was a top priority.

Minutes after this photo was snapped, John demonstrated how safe his Indigen Armor vehicles were by riding in this armored car as it was fired on by heavy-caliber weapons, and coming out without a scratch.

Here's Chris Campbell, at about age twenty, with his long locks and brand-new wheels. The sandals, man, the sandals.

"What's special about Chris," said his friend and fellow North Carolinian Randy Kelley, "is not that he's larger than life. It's kind of like he *is* life."

Chris loved the outdoors; to him the ocean was a second home. Here he is on the boardwalk: "Welcome to my world."

Chris had an amazing ability to be at home wherever he was. No matter where *here* was at the moment, he never seemed to want to be anywhere else.

Campbell never lost his temper and always had a smile on his face, no matter what. Here he is on the beach with his daughter, Sam—who has clearly inherited that famous Chris smile.

Heath Robinson was one of my Team Three teammates at Echo Platoon, when we went into Afghanistan immediately after 9/11 and cleared the massive cave-complex training grounds at Zhawar Kili. We ended up in the winter in some seriously high altitudes—with virtually no cold-weather gear.

Talk about climate contrast: from our deployment in the frigid mountains of northern Afghanistan to a different platoon serving in the desert of Iraq.

Heath had an insatiable appetite for self-improvement; his work ethic became legendary among the teams. Here he is, decked out in camo, eating up the intense training of sniper school.

Top: Heath's nickname was Hollywood, because of both his good looks and his love of movies. The guys called this photo of Heath in full battle gear with helo in background his "Hollywood shot."

Right: Heath in Afghanistan, ready for a priority mission, not long before the downing of Extortion 17 in August 2011.

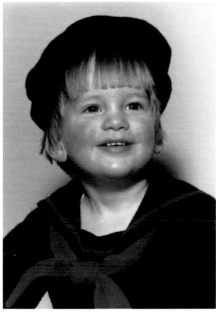

Courtesy of Kathy Tumilson

Even at age eighteen months, JT Tumilson was already a lady charmer.

A friend once described JT as a "human Labrador: smart, athletic, and you want him to be with you everywhere you go"—an inside joke, because JT's one constant companion was his chocolate Lab, Hawkeye.

Courtesy of Kathy Tumilson

Courtesy of Scott McMeekan

JT's brother-in-law Scott McMeekan snapped this shot of JT on what would turn out to be his last visit home for Christmas, eight months before Extortion 17 was shot down in Afghanistan in August 2011.

At his funeral, JT's faithful Lab, Hawkeye, walked down the center aisle, lay down in front of the coffin, and didn't budge for the rest of the service. Within days this photo went viral, capturing an anguish over the loss of so many of our finest warriors that resonated nationally.

This is a ceremony I've come to know too well: On August 19, 2011, SEAL team brothers kneel in a gesture of respect and grief after pounding their Tridents into JT's casket.

Top: Everyone's best friend: Glen Doherty poses for a family snap-shot with his sister, Kate; Kate's boys; and his mom, Barbara.

Middle: At one point in our crazy death-defying cross-country trip in 2005, after we'd lost communi-cations and visibility and the plane's wings were starting to ice up, Glen turned to me, laughed, and said, "Hey, at least we've got each other."

Bottom: The Doherty clan—Glen, Kate, and Greg—knew how to have good times together and did so every chance they got.

Long after we'd both been through the teams, Glen and I were still constantly hanging out together—especially if it involved the outdoors. Here we are getting ready for a one-and-a-half-mile swim event in 2011.

Glen and I had a blast together with fans at a book-signing event in Times Square, New York City, August 2012. It was the last time I saw him. A few weeks later he was killed in Benghazi.

capabilities on our helos, with better and/or additional countermeasures?

Granted, they may not have had 100 percent accuracy on that MANPAD observation. But there was enough to put it in the damn report. If it'd been me, I sure as hell would have mentioned it. How many more helicopters have been shot down between June 2005 and now—including the helo carrying Chris, Heath, JT, and more than two dozen others—that potentially might *not* have been shot down had we looked squarely at the intelligence from the ground and adjusted our rules and procedures accordingly?

They held a funeral service for the lost heroes of Extortion 17 at Arlington, where they buried all the Americans from the crash together. My old Golf Platoon teammate Mike Ritland attended the service, and while he was there he suddenly thought about Dave Scott and his tragic passing in Guam nine years earlier, in part because Dave had also been buried at Arlington. "The shittiest thing about Dave's death," Mike says, "was that none of us could go to the funeral because we were all on deployment out in the Philippines at the time." Mike had felt awful that he couldn't be there for Kat on that day back in 2002. And yet, in the nine years since, he had never visited the grave site.

He says he still can't explain exactly why that was. He doesn't need to explain it to me.

When the ceremony was over, Mike started walking. Before long he found himself at Dave Scott's grave site. It was nearing five o'clock, but in that late August D.C. afternoon the heat still hung around Mike like a canopy. Like Guam.

Nobody else was around, not even a car driving by, just humid, hovering silence. He stood for a bit, then knelt down and placed a SEAL Team Three coin and a SEAL Trident down on Dave's grave site, where they joined the small cluster of Marine Marathon finishers' medals.

"I talked to Dave for a few minutes," recalls Mike. "Busted his balls for a bit. Then got up and went on my way."

A lot of time had passed since Dave Scott's death in 2002, and even more since Mike Bearden's two years before that. I'd lost quite a few more friends over those years, and now so many at once—not only Chris and Heath and JT but more than a dozen other good men, some of whom I knew in passing, and all of whom I knew in one way or another, if only by reputation. It's a close-knit community.

But still, I didn't go to Arlington.

At this point I still hadn't attended a single memorial service.

Not long after the crash, I wrote a blog post honoring the guys who were on that helo. In the post I mentioned how Heath and I had been friends in Afghanistan. Someone, an unidentified teams guy, wrote a comment on the post: "Some friend—you didn't even go to the funeral."

To this day I don't know who wrote those words, but they burned deep. The thing is, we all have to deal with loss and grief in our own way. I didn't show up for the funeral, but that didn't mean Heath and Chris and JT and all the others weren't weighing heavy on my heart.

At the time of the helo crash, my book *The Red Circle* was about to be published, and I was thinking about what I should work on next. The loss of so many friends in one terrible event planted a seed that took shape over the following year and would eventually become the book you hold in your hands. In 2012 my writing partner and I drew up a proposal, signed a contract with a publisher, and started work on the manuscript.

I never imagined that before it was over I would be writing about my best friend, Glen.

EVERYONE'S
BEST FRIEND

GLEN DOHERTY

The first time I saw Glen Doherty, he was relaxing in a parked Humvee, reading a book, and I was on the edge of physical collapse.

I remember the moment like a snapshot, because it struck me right then how ironic it was. Here we were, the toughest of the tough, baddest of the bad, strapping young specimens on our way to becoming Navy SEALs, and what was this guy doing? Sitting there reading some piece of classical literature like a third-year English lit student. And here was the ironic part: My first thought was, *Hey, another one*. Because reading was one of my great loves, too—classic novels, popular page-turners, memoirs, business books, you name it. Being a voracious reader was something Glen and I had in common— as I would soon learn, one of many things we had in common. Maybe we both sensed that.

In any case, there we were: him perched in his comfortable Humvee, me on my last legs, one of the few men still standing in the final stretch of a brutal fourteen-mile forced run in full gear in the scorching midsummer California desert, which on a cool day was close to a hundred degrees. And this wasn't a cool day. Out of a class of seventy-two guys, barely a dozen of us were still vertical.

Actually, I wasn't exactly vertical either. Both my legs had just seized up and I had dropped like a sack of cement.

Glen glanced up from his book and grinned at me. "How ya doin'? Ya look like shit."

I did look like shit. I *felt* like shit.

It was the summer of 1998, toward the end of our STT session at postapocalyptic Niland, and this was that same fourteen-mile ordeal that Mike Bearden breezed through and that just about killed the rest of us. Of course, our instructors didn't want it to *literally* kill us. They just wanted to take us as close to that brink as they could without any of us actually tipping over the edge. Which was why Glen was there. Glen was a Navy medic, or corpsman, about to go through STT himself, and right now attached to our class as support staff, on hand to make sure we didn't die from heatstroke or dehydration in the inhuman conditions at Niland.

I didn't know this guy, but something about him stood out. For one thing, he seemed like he was in a perpetual great mood, his face always wearing an easy smile. Not an evil grin or a fuck-you sneer (we had plenty of those in the group), just a genuine, good-natured smile. Which stood out even more for a corpsman.

Most corpsmen tended to have a pretty pissed-off attitude at that point, stemming from the fact that they were stuck in a sort of built-in career rut. Their path to earning their SEAL Trident was at least six months longer than it was for the rest of us. While we went directly on to STT right out of BUD/S, corpsmen first had to go through a six-month training course out at Fort Bragg: the Special Operations medical course, also known as 18 Delta. Glen had actually gone through BUD/S well before the rest of us—but here we were, plowing on through STT, which Glen hadn't even started yet. Like all corpsmen, he was anxious to get started. Still, it didn't seem to have put a chip on his shoulder.

Even in the midst of the excruciating pain, as I tried to get my seized-up leg muscles working again, I could see that he was a genuine guy, someone you could get to know and trust right away. There's a great line from *The Shawshank Redemption*, when Red (Morgan Freeman) first meets Andy Dufresne (Tim Robbins) in prison:

> He had a quiet way about him, a walk and a talk that just wasn't normal around here. He strolled like a man in a park without a care or worry in the world, like he had on an invisible coat that would shield him from this place. Yeah, I think it would be fair to say . . . I liked Andy from the start.

This guy was like that. Like Andy Dufresne, he had a quiet smile on his face, like he was mostly here but a part of him was somewhere else, listening to the punch line of a joke the rest of us hadn't heard yet. It was just a fleeting impression, though, and in the remaining days of STT I barely got to know him, let alone to sense that he would become one of the most influential people in my life. I was too busy getting my ass kicked.

Glen helped me to my feet, got some water in me, and watched me take off again to make those last few miles before collapsing for the night.

. . .

A few months later, STT now behind me, I was out surfing off the San Diego coast. This beautiful tube opened up in front of me. I pulled into it, and in the next moment it collapsed around me—in surfer's terms, it *closed out*. My board flew up out of control and I took a rail in the head, banged myself up pretty bad.

I got myself back onto the beach to assess the situation. My face was covered in blood. Probably no more than an inch-and-a-half gash, but head wounds bleed like a son of a bitch.

I had a few choices: I could go in to the naval hospital, the Navy's version of the ER. But as SEALs we had our own medical clinic, each team with its own medical station. Much easier: faster service, less paperwork. Hell, all I needed was a few off-the-record stitches. Most SEALs I know have very few entries in their medical records—as few as possible, in fact. I climbed into my car and drove myself over to Team Three medical, parked, and walked in bleeding all over the place.

There were two medics on call: a guy I didn't know, and Glen.

I wasn't that well versed in Special Operations yet, but I'd seen enough to know that there were two kinds of medics in the service: One is the guy who is skilled but treats you like a farm animal. He looks you over, punches a needle in your arm, and says, "I gave you a local; now shut the fuck up and hold still while I stitch you up." They might be great guys otherwise. I've had quite a few friends who fall into the brutal-medic category, and I'd trust my life to them on the battlefield. (In fact, I *have*.) I'd just rather not have them sewing me up if I have the luxury of choice.

Even without knowing Glen all that well, it was obvious he was the other kind of corpsman: the kind who has a genuine knack for it, who gravitates to the job because he actually wants to take care of people. *And* animals.

When Glen was a kid and adults would ask him what he wanted to be when he grew up, he would answer, "A veterinarian." From the earliest age, he had a love of animals. He and his siblings were always taking in strays. One day Glen and his sister, Kate, found a mouse and sneaked it up to the third-floor attic. They named it Speedy and kept it in secret for days, until their mom caught them smuggling food upstairs. She let them keep the little guy.

Not long after that, Glen adopted a stray black-and-white cat he named Raisin (for reasons known only to Glen). Raisin was a street cat, mean and tough as nails. That crazy tom located Speedy without difficulty, and that was the end of Speedy. A few months later the kids got another kitten. Raisin killed it that first night. When Kate would try to pet Raisin, he would bite her. This cat was one bad son of a bitch, the nastiest cat the kids had ever seen. But Glen loved him, and Raisin loved Glen. He was Glen's cat and nobody else's.

Glen was the same way with people. There wasn't *anyone* he couldn't relate to and get along with. Of course, I didn't know any of this until much later, when we got to be good friends. But I knew enough to make sure it was Glen who stitched me up, and not the other guy.

I sat on the table at Team Three medical, and he went to work.

"Okay," he said, "I'm going to give you a local, and then I'm gonna irrigate this wound. . . ." As he worked he explained what he was doing, step by step. "Okay," I heard him say, "you're good to go." Before I knew it, I was out of there with seven stitches on my head and a new friend.

As I got to know Glen better, I learned more about what his 18 Delta training had been like.

"Imagine being in a dark room," he told me one day. "Earsplitting rock music blaring over loudspeakers, strobe lights going on and off. Guy on the floor in front of you with a gunshot wound. You have to find his vein in the dark, give him an IV, do it right—and do it fast, because his life is ebbing away. Okay, it's not actually a guy. It's a goat. But guess what: If that goat dies, you don't graduate."

It might be a goat, or a pig, or some other animal. Sometimes it was a gunshot wound, other times a severed limb or some other trauma with equally fatal potential. Not for the faint of heart.

"Also not very popular with the PETA set," he added. "But it's damn good training, and it saves guys' lives in the field."

After Fort Bragg they were shipped to New York City for some on-the-job training: riding around in civilian ambulances and working the ER.

"They sent us to the worst neighborhoods," he told me, "where drug-related violence and gang warfare are an everyday thing. I treated a lot of stabbings and gunshot wounds."

Glen told me about one 911 call they responded to where a man had called in and said he couldn't get out of his bed, and it was an emergency. They drove to the address and hoofed it up the five- or six-story walk-up, and once they crashed into the guy's apartment, they saw why he couldn't get out of bed.

"Dude"—Glen shook his head and gave an incredulous

laugh—"this guy was *beyond* fat. He was morbidly obese. I mean, he couldn't *move*."

He paused for a second, trying to find the words to describe the scene.

"Stacks of old rotting magazines, delivery boxes, mostly empty food containers all over the place, shit piled everywhere . . . and this unbelievable stench. It was like that scene out of *Se7en*—you know, the murdered guy who exemplified the sin of sloth? This was that guy."

Glen and his teammates had to hoist the obese man out of his bed and carry him down all those flights of stairs.

"I saw a lot of ugly things in 18 Delta," he said. "That was the worst. But hey, you know? We had to help the guy."

A few days before receiving my Trident that fall, I learned I was being assigned to Golf Platoon. Being assigned to a platoon is a kind of draft-pick process, much the way it works with a pro sports team. Each platoon had its own reputation, some decidedly better than others. We all had high hopes for which platoon we'd be assigned to.

Golf Platoon was one of the best. Glen was there, and so was my BUD/S classmate Mike Ritland, who was living at the time in that one-bedroom guesthouse behind the little house I was renting in San Diego. Mike, who today is a renowned dog trainer and author of *Trident K9 Warriors*, a bestselling book about SEAL dogs, tells a story about being—forgive the expression, Mike—sick as a dog in that house.

Understand, when you're in the SEALs, you don't call in sick. If you think you're sick you go in anyway. If the officers in charge say you're too sick to be there, *then* you go home. But this time Mike got so sick that he literally couldn't go in.

He'd gotten food poisoning from some bad clams, and spent days puking continuously and uncontrollably. To make things worse, none of us *knew* he was sick. He was back there in that little cottage by himself with no phone. He couldn't go for help. He couldn't even walk.

"I would crawl slowly from my bed to my bathroom," he says, "where I would collapse on the floor for an hour or two before I could manage to crawl back to my bed. After a few days of this, I was so dehydrated, I knew I was going to die."

And then, like an angel of mercy appearing out of nowhere, Glen came bursting through the door with two five-hundred-milliliter bags of IV fluids and a satchel of meds. He got some fluids into Mike, got him cleaned up a little and put together. Over the next few days he came back a few more times to check up on Mike and make sure he was okay.

To this day Mike says he has no idea how Glen knew he was at home dying. "Maybe he noticed I hadn't shown up for quarters for a few days and figured it out. All I know is, he saved my life."

As I got to know Glen a little better I learned something about him I hadn't seen at first: Beneath that affable, unflappable exterior there beat the heart of a freaking perfectionist.

Glen, or "Bub," as we all called him, excelled at everything he put his mind and body to. It wasn't that he was a naturally gifted athlete. He was a slender guy, not built especially like a born jock. But he was driven. His childhood pal Sean explains it perfectly: "Glen was the one who was willing to put in the work."

In those years between STT and deploying overseas, we did a lot of surfing off the Coronado coast. I was practically born in the water and spent most of my teenage years working on a dive boat. Not Glen. He was a gifted skier—as Sean puts it, "Watching Glen on skis was seeing poetry in motion"—but he was no natural-born surfer. In fact, he honestly wasn't that good at it. But he had more damn fun surfing than anyone else I've ever known, and he poured himself into it hard enough to get himself to the point of competence.

Glen never seemed to need much sleep. He was always the last one to crash at night and the first to get up in the morning. If he wasn't heading out for a run, he was in the kitchen cooking everyone breakfast—or getting everyone else up to run. He would be up at dawn after a night of major partying, when everyone was still hungover, calling out, "Okay, everybody, we're goin' on a six-mile run and then gonna lift some weights!" Everyone else would be groaning, "Jesus, no—c'mon, Glen . . ." but off he'd go. He called it "sweating the demons out." You work hard, you play hard, and then you get back to work on yourself again—hard. That was not only Glen's modus operandi—it was also his working definition of life as a SEAL.

Guys enlist in the service and join the teams for all sorts of reasons. For some, like Matt Axelson or Heath Robinson, it's in their bloodlines. Dave Scott wanted to jump out of planes and blow things up. Chris Campbell wanted to see the world. But Glen? According to his friends and family, for him the idea of becoming a SEAL was more or less a bolt from the blue. Glen's sister, Kate, says she was talking with Glen one day and he told her something that surprised her. "If nothing else comes up by the time I'm twenty-five," he commented, "I'll become a Navy SEAL." *A Navy SEAL?* she thought. *Where did* that *come from?*

In fact, it came from Costa Rica. That summer he and a buddy had spent some time there, and they happened to meet a group of SEALs who were doing the same thing they were: hanging out and surfing. Back home Glen had been having a tough time carving out a career as a skier. His buddy Sean had by now become a sponsored pro snowboarder, but while pro snowboarding was on the rise in the mid-nineties, skiing was at an ebb, and as good as Glen was, he still didn't see any prospects of getting serious sponsorship.

Fine, he thought. *If this doesn't happen in the next year, I'll become a Navy SEAL.*

Sure enough, when he turned twenty-five he enlisted. But it wasn't that "nothing else had come up." *Everything* else had come up. He'd hitchhiked across the country (following the Grateful Dead, no less), worked in a microbrewery, hung out in boxing gyms. . . . It seemed there was nothing Glen hadn't done. Not only was he an expert skier, but by that time he was also a skilled whitewater-rafting instructor, an accomplished triathlete, an experienced chef, and an excellent writer. He became such a skillful medic that a top brain surgeon offered to pay his way through physician's assistant (PA) school if Glen would come work for him. An A student throughout his school years, he excelled at everything he did. He could have done almost anything. But being the best wasn't enough for him. He had to be the best of the best.

And he was. In BUD/S, we had a designation for the top graduate in the class: Honor Man. Over time the idea spread to most other courses as well. In practically every class we went through together, Glen was Honor Man.

. . .

It was in sniper school that Glen and I became inseparable. Since we were paired up as shooter-spotter partners, we spent the next three months training together, eating together, drinking together, shooting, sweating, stressing, and cursing together. Our fates in the course were tied to each other. In those three months the two of us forged a bond of trust and friendship that went deeper than bone marrow. Over a lot of late-night campfire hours, we also learned a lot about each other's childhoods and backgrounds.

Glen grew up with a typical suburban New England childhood, happily riding bikes and playing soccer in the street. The Doherty family lived on a street named Glen Road (I kid you not), right across the street from a patch of woods called Glen Green, where they spent a lot of time wandering through the woods in a pack with their friends across the street, Chad, Tim, and Nathaniel Haskell.

The Glen Road house was the social center of the neighborhood. All the kids seemed to congregate there. Part of it was that Glen's mom, Barbara, was so welcoming and tolerant and didn't seem to mind kids coming and going and traipsing through their home. Part of it was some sort of gravitational field that Glen seemed to generate. Kids just wanted to be around him.

When Glen left college to become a professional ski bum in Utah, he got an apartment together with a few friends that generated that same social pull. Glen spent his early twenties working at Snowbird (where they've since named his favorite off-trail run after him), and for all those years, their little apartment was where everyone hung out.

The same thing happened once again during our eighteen-month workup after STT. Glen and his girlfriend, Sonja, got a cool little house in Coronado, and people were drawn to hang out there as if it were the only watering hole in an 1880s Western cowboy town.

And now here we were, together in sniper school, camping out in the middle of nowhere, and son of a bitch if Glen's tent didn't somehow exert that same damn gravitational pull. For the twenty-six of us who started that course, putting in those grueling days with hours-long stretches of intense, unbroken concentration and the threat of failure hanging constantly over our heads, Glen's tent became the after-hours social hub: the Glen Road of sniper school.

That actually started every day before dawn, when Glen became the focal point of attention in a not so positive way. Here's how I described the morning scene in *The Red Circle*:

> The range had a nice little grass campground complete with a kitchen and a restrooms/shower area. All the students were instructed to bring a tent and kit. Most of the guys traveled pretty light. I take just what I need, and it all fits in my pack. Guys in the teams had a saying "Pack light and mooch." My saying was "Don't pack light—pack right." Not Glen, though. As I soon learned, Glen liked to travel in comfort, which meant plenty of extras. He was like a one-man gypsy camp. He must have gone out and bought the biggest tent he could find at the local Kmart; that thing could have slept a family of ten. He had three fuel-burning lanterns, a radio, a coffeemaker, a generator—it was out of control.
>
> We were partners, so my tent was right next to his. I love Glen like a brother, but this was torture.

That son of a bitch would be up and about for a solid hour before the rest of us even started thinking about opening our eyes, and once he was up it was nearly impossible to stay asleep because his gypsy encampment lit up the whole side of my tent. First I was awakened by the blinding white glow and steady hum of his Coleman exploration power lanterns. Then the sounds would start: his percolating coffeepot, then some sort of eighties rock music blaring through his earphones, which he thought we couldn't hear but in fact only made him even more oblivious to the extent of the racket he was making, messing around with all his stuff, clattering around and getting his coffee ready, burping and farting but not hearing himself because he had those earphones in, then followed by his electric toothbrush, endless loud gargle, and the invariable lengthy punctuating spit that made us all groan. After a week or so of this daily routine, the guys began referring to Glen's morning ablutions as "Chernobyl."

If I had my choice, I would pull myself out of sleep maybe twenty minutes before we had to muster up, giving myself just enough time to brush my teeth, throw some water on my face, and grab my gear. But no. I tried for days, but it was not possible. Finally I succumbed and started letting Glen be my alarm clock.

In many ways Glen and I were very different, almost opposites. He was always a popular kid, the kind of guy nobody could dislike, often playing the role of negotiator and peacemaker. I was a fighter, always getting into trouble and taking things to extremes. He was Massachusetts. I was California. He lived in one place his whole childhood, in a stable suburban home in the kind of close New England neighborhood where nobody locks their doors. My family was restless and always on the move, which meant my sister and I were constantly being uprooted and having to start all over again, getting into new fights and making new friends—friends we would eventually lose.

Regardless of those differences, though, Glen and I had clicked immediately, and those things we held in common forged the foundation of a lifelong friendship. We both loved being outdoors. We both had a passion for doing something as well as you can possibly do it. We both had zero tolerance for bullshit.

And we both had deeply troubled relationships with our fathers.

Glen's parents split up when he was nine, casting a pall over that idyllic childhood, a dark cloud that never dispersed. His older brother, Greg, remembers their parents sitting the kids down on the front steps and breaking the news that they were separating. Glen burst into tears. A few days later their dad pulled up in a truck and parked out front. Greg helped load up their dad's stuff to take to his new house, but Glen refused; he ran across the street and into the woods even before his dad showed up.

"He held that grudge against Dad forever," says Greg. "He never entirely let it go."

Ben Doherty's new place wasn't that far away, and he remained in the Doherty kids' lives. For years afterward, though, Glen and he had a tough time getting along. The conflict between them simmered to a boiling point in his senior year of high school, when they got into a big fight. (Over what, nobody seems to remember). Glen decided enough was enough: He walked out of the house in protest and moved in with a friend's family down the street. Which was kind of fascinating to me, when he told me about it— because it was at about that same age that my dad threw *me* out of the house. (Since we were docked off Tahiti in the South Pacific at the time, it's more accurate to say he threw me off the boat.) It was one of those things, like our obsession with reading, that we had in common.

Which made it even more amazing to me that Glen got along so well with my father. In fact, it was Glen who brought about a completely unexpected reconciliation between the two of us.

In early 2000, a few months before we learned we were going into sniper school, Glen and a buddy of his visited my dad's place in Wyoming with me to go skiing for a few days.

One day we were sitting at a table in the lodge after a few hours of skiing, putting back a few beers. Glen was regaling us with tales of his experiences as a medic, and the conversation turned to the topic of lifesaving. Glen described how he'd saved a guy in a fancy restaurant in Park City when the guy almost choked to death. Glen had his pocketknife out, ready to cut the guy's neck open and trache him, though it didn't quite come to that. The conversation went on like that for a while, when all of a sudden my dad, who'd hardly spoken the whole time we'd been there, came out with eight words that almost made me spit out my beer.

"Yeah, you know, Brandon saved *my* life once."

He and I had never talked about this. I was seventeen at

the time, working on the dive boat back in California that I'd made my home after being banished from the family boat, and my dad had visited to do a little scuba diving. While attempting to surface, he got himself mired in a bed of kelp, then panicked and spit out his regulator. I happened to be on rescue diver duty, so I dived in, swam the three or four hundred yards to where he was, and yanked his ass out of there.

The event had created an uneasy awkwardness between the two of us ever since it happened, an unspoken elephant in the middle of the living room. And now, all of a sudden here he was, my tough, taciturn dad, spilling his guts about what had happened and how he'd felt at the time. Jack Webb with tears in his eyes, telling these strangers about how his kid had saved his hide and how he'd never forget it.

I was dumbfounded. I'd never seen my dad so vulnerable. And why? Because he was talking to Glen.

That was how Glen was. Anybody could open up to him, and everybody did.

By the time 9/11 happened I had been moved to Echo Platoon, and within days of the attack I was on my way to Afghanistan. When I came back six months and a lifetime later, two big things had changed: Glen had gotten married. And I'd become a father.

Glen had strongly resisted the commitment of marriage. He and Sonja had even broken up over this issue at one point. But after 9/11 it was a crazy, grab-your-loved-ones time. He knew he would be deployed overseas before long, and it just felt like the right thing to do. So he caved, and off they went to town hall to get married while I was chasing down bad guys and caches of contraband in the caves of the Hindu Kush.

Glen's obsession with perfection extended to relationships. In any area of interest or aspiration, from food to skiing to jobs and careers, he had his list of exacting, carefully worked-out criteria, and that went for women, too. If you asked Glen what he was looking for in a girl, he would reel off a whole inventory of necessary qualities: "She has to be beautiful and fit, to challenge me, be witty, be natural, not wear a lot of makeup, and be able to run a triathlon, and . . ."

We'd say, "Glen, give me a freaking break. That human being doesn't exist." But he had his standards and wasn't backing down. The problem was, he had that same impossibly high set of standards for what it meant to be a husband and father. His own dad had flunked that test, in Glen's eyes, and in time so would Glen. I know he never forgave his dad; I wonder if he ever completely forgave himself.

Still, while he never did have any children of his own, kids took to him the same way animals did, the same way *everyone* did.

A few days after I got back home from Afghanistan I had Glen over to the house to meet my six-month-old son, Jackson. The funny thing was, I'd been home for only a few days and my wife, Gabriele, hadn't really started trusting me with our son yet. It was as if she were afraid I might drop and break him. She'd go out to the grocery store and take Jackson with her, rather than leave him with me. But she had no problem letting Glen hold him. Jackson crawled all over Uncle Glen like he'd known him all his life.

After a while Gabriele and Jackson took off somewhere,

and I sat down with Glen and told him about my time in Afghanistan. We talked well into the night. I told him everything, stories I've never told anyone else, showed him pictures I've never shown anyone else, and never will.

War gets ugly; don't ever let anyone tell you otherwise.

The following year it was Glen who was shipped out to the Middle East, where he was part of Shock and Awe from stem to stern, starting with the split-second-timing VBSS boarding and dismantling of Saddam's oil platforms on the eve of the invasion, on to the rescue of Jessica Lynch (the first successful rescue of an American POW since World War II), to the taking of Saddam's palace and the fall of Tikrit, which signaled the end of the Battle of Iraq and led to President Bush's now-infamous "Mission Accomplished" press conference on the USS *Abraham Lincoln*. Glen was there for all of it.

For me, being part of the post-9/11 operation in Afghanistan had been a hell of an education, and it packed an awful lot of experience into six short months. The invasion of Iraq was that same experience for Glen, and he saw his share of the realities of war. When he returned to the States he came over to my place again, and we did the same kind of debriefing we'd done on my return from Afghanistan, only this time it was him sharing the stories with me.

Throughout our years in the service, Glen and I hung out every chance we got. We drank together, went surfing together, and stayed up late into the night talking together. More than anything else, we pursued our lifelong passion for flying together.

With all the ocean training and "frogman" thing, it's easy

to forget that the "A" in SEAL stands for *air*. All my life I'd wanted to be a pilot, and so had Glen. Fresh out of high school he enrolled in Embry-Riddle Aeronautical University in Arizona and earned a bachelor's in aeronautics.

In early 2005 I bought a little 1981 Cessna 172 over the Internet. The guy I was buying it from lived out in Illinois, so I asked Glen to fly there with me and help me bring it home. This was February and a bad snowstorm was moving in, so we had limited time to get this sucker out of there.

By this time Glen was out of the service (though I was still in), and he had just finished his instrument qual; I was about to finish mine. We were flying a lot, so we were both pretty current. We were also cocky and overconfident, as SEALs tend to be.

Arriving at the airport in the evening, we decided we'd collect the plane right away and get the hell out of there. It was dark and cloudy out, with the storm system on its way in, but we figured we were charged up and ready to go. Just as we were about to leave the pilot's lounge and head to the plane, this old-timer walks over to our table and says, "Hey, you two fellas the ones just bought old Bob's Cessna?"

Yeah, we said, that was us.

"You fellas really think it's a good idea to take that plane out tonight? Having never flown it before? In this kinda weather?"

We looked at each other. The old guy had a point. After he left I turned to Glen and said, "What the fuck were we thinking?" He grinned and didn't say anything. There's a saying in aviation: "There are bold pilots and old pilots, but no old bold pilots." We stayed in Illinois that night.

The next morning we got up at dawn, filed our flight plan

for our first leg to Oklahoma, grabbed some coffee, hopped into the plane, and took off. From eight hundred feet up it was IMC (instrument meteorological conditions), pilotspeak for "too overcast to see," but we knew once we got high enough we would break out of the cloud layer.

As we started climbing, we discovered that our radio didn't work. We were hearing the tower okay, but they weren't hearing us; we'd somehow lost the ability to transmit.

Okay: no visibility and no communications.

At about five thousand feet I glanced out my window and said, "Hey, Glen, I don't know how to tell you this, but look." He looked over past me, out my window. Rime icing—the frosty white ice that forms when water vapor freezes to the surfaces of cold objects—was starting to form on the wing struts. Flying in ice, in a plane that isn't certified to fly in ice: not good. If we descended back through the cloud layer we would just keep picking up more ice. If we kept climbing and broke out, the ice would probably burn off. We had to keep climbing.

No visibility, no communications, and a plane that was icing up.

"Shit," I said.

We looked at each other and laughed. Glen said, "Hey, at least we've got each other. If we're gonna go, we go together."

At about seven thousand feet, the cloud cover broke. IFR (instrument flight rules) are when you fly east you fly at odd altitudes, and when you fly west you fly at even altitudes, for clean traffic separation. At VFR (visual flight rules) it's even plus five hundred, but this was an IFR plane. We flew at eight thousand feet all the way to Oklahoma, the whole way trying to figure out what the hell was wrong with our radio. We happened to have a little Garmin aviation GPS with us. That damn thing probably saved our lives.

As we flew into Tulsa we settled into our precision-instrument approach, when we made another fun discovery: Our glide scope didn't work. Oh, cool. Now we were executing a precision-instrument landing without precision instruments, and no radio. And it was still cloudy. I pulled out a little handheld radio I'd happened to bring along. That would have to serve.

Nothing to do but just fly the damn thing in.

We broke out of the clouds in the center of the runway, midfield, right smack over the tower. A voice came over the radio: "Hey, you've only got about two hundred feet of runway left; you want to circle around and then land?"

I looked at Glen with a question on my face. He looked back and said, "Dude, I am so stressed, I'm puttin' this fucking thing down right now."

And we did: just planted it on the deck like an aircraft-carrier landing, which is to say, like a dog taking a dump. Thump! there it is. Stopped short with less than fifty feet of runway in front of us—and taxied in with just enough reserve gas to make it.

Once we were on the ground the radio worked perfectly. It wasn't till we eventually got back to San Diego that we figured out what had happened: The antennae weren't grounded properly, so as long as we were on the ground everything worked fine, but once we were in the air, no dice. Good to know. Would have been even better to have known *before* flying halfway across the country.

We refueled and took off again. After a total of sixteen and a half hours in the air we stayed overnight in New Mexico, then made the final leg home.

Glen and I did a lot of flying over the years, but what we really wanted to do was fly a single-engine plane clear around the world. The speed record for that particular feat was still quite breakable, and we knew we could crush it. But we never got the chance. I'd still love to do it. I just don't know whether there's anyone I'd trust enough as a flying partner—anyone other than Glen.

In 2006, a year after our cross-country adventure in the little Cessna, I left the service, and the first thing I did was follow Glen's footsteps (and John Zinn's) into the world of private security contracting. Glen, as usual, knew the right people, and he helped me get my application fast-tracked so that by the time I left the service, I already had a deployment date set in the shadowy world of private-contract security work, or Global Response Staff (GRS).

This is a realm most people don't know much about, but private-contract security work is a noble calling that gave people like John Zinn, Glen, and me the opportunity to keep serving our country and making the world a safer place even after taking off the uniform.

In the Special Operations community, we have a belief that there are three types of people in the world. The *wolves* are what most would call "evil people." They are the rapists and murderers, the psychopaths and extremists who prey on the weak and use violence and others' fear to achieve their goals. In the twentieth century they stood on stages and commanded armies, if they were lucky. In the twenty-first, they hide in the shadows, guide planes into skyscrapers, and delude their recruits into blowing themselves up in public places.

Then there are the sheep—good people, everyday people who go about their lives, able to do so in safety only because they are protected from the wolves. For the most part, they are not aware of the wolves, or that they are being protected from them. They may not even really believe that there *are* wolves out there, ready to cause them harm. But there are.

And sheepdogs are acutely aware of it.

Sheepdogs can look like wolves, and may at times even be mistaken for them, but they serve the opposite cause. They exist not to prey on sheep but to preserve them, to protect those who cannot protect themselves, as Mike Bearden explained it to his dad. They are here for one purpose: to look after the safety of the flock.

Here's an easy way to understand the difference between sheepdogs and everyone else. Most people, when they hear about a terrorist event or violent attack, think, "Thank God I wasn't in that movie theater or on that plane." A sheepdog hears about the same event and says, "Damn—I wish I'd *been* there!" Why? Because maybe he could have done something to stop it from happening.

As Heath Robinson's sig line said, most of us are able to go about our lives in relative safety only because there are "rough men standing ready in the night to visit violence on those who would do us harm." Sheepdogs are those rough men. That was who Glen was, whether or not he happened to be an active-duty Navy SEAL at the time.

For my part, I did some of this work in Iraq, where I ran

all sorts of missions, from the insanely dangerous to the dangerously insane—missions I can't talk about but which, if I could, would make for some pretty colorful, edge-of-your-seat action flicks.

I did that routine twice, for a stretch of a few months each. Glen had by then been doing it for a few years, and he kept doing it long after I stopped, traveling to work in the world's hottest hot spots and most explosive situations. The most dangerous scene he ever encountered, he told me, was not in the Middle East or Africa but in Mexico City, where he worked with a man who didn't seem to fully grasp the over-the-top risks he was taking.

Glen was furious with the guy's carelessness. Because of his arrogant refusal to listen to the advice of experience, he was endangering a lot of other lives.

"Look, dude," Glen told the man, "if you keep going like this you're going to get whacked. It's not a matter of *if*. It's only a question of *when*."

In the summer of 2010, Glen turned forty, and his siblings and friends pulled a "surprise" birthday party for him, the word in quotes because of course he knew about it ahead of time. I don't think there was a party anywhere on planet Earth since 1970 that Glen didn't know about ahead of time. Still, he did a great job of acting surprised.

He did a less than perfect job of acting happy. His marriage had fallen apart not long before this, and it was eating at him. On the one hand, he relished the freedom (which was more or less why it didn't work out in the first place). He and Sonja had a little sign on their Encinitas house that said, THE DOHERTYS. The first time I visited there after the divorce went through, I saw that Glen had crossed out the s so that it now read simply, THE DOHERTY. He got the biggest kick out of that.

At the same time, he was completely torn up about it. I think it was less the fact that that they weren't together anymore and more that he'd failed. Glen hated failure. As tolerant as he was—and he was one of the most tolerant people I've ever known—he had no tolerance for failure. Especially *this* failure. This was what his dad had done.

By this time he had been doing this private-contract security work for years, and everyone who knew him and loved him could see that it was wearing on him. It was wearing on the whole country. We'd been at war for nearly a decade, the longest stretch of continuous warfare in our nation's young history. And it was sapping us—financially, emotionally, some would argue (and I would not disagree) even morally. Glen was showing the signs of that wear.

I cannot honestly say he was looking seriously at alternatives, at least not yet. But his friends were certainly looking for him, me included. I was working hard on the Wind Zero project and brought Glen in as a minority partner. He became intensely involved for a while, not only helping with the fund-raising effort but also managing training and consulting contracts. When a large contract came in I could hand it over to Glen and sleep like a baby at night, knowing he'd take impeccable care of the customers. When I started work on my first book, *21st Century Sniper* (later rereleased as *Navy SEAL Sniper*), Glen was my coauthor. When I took a cherry executive position for a major defense firm after Wind Zero collapsed to make ends meet, I tried my best to get Glen to look at taking one as well.

And these were not his only career options. On a surfing trip to Mexico in 2009, a buddy of ours got smashed into some rocks and had his spine pierced. He needed emergency surgery. There was no one around to do that but us. As it happened, one of our party was Sohaib Kureshi, a brilliant Pakistani brain surgeon. (Note to self: When surfing off-country, always bring along a brilliant surfer brain surgeon.) We tossed our friend onto a picnic table at the place where we were staying, after stopping off at the only nearby store for beer and painkillers, and turned to Glen—who had his medic kit on hand, as always. Glen loaded our buddy with morphine, irrigated the puncture site, and proceeded to help Sohaib do the delicate surgery. "If he's interested in doing it," Sohaib told us after it was all over, "Glen's got a brilliant medical career ahead of him." (For two weeks every year Glen ran a medical clinic on Tavarua Island, a destination surf resort off the coast of Fiji.)

Glen had looked at all these options, and there was something attractive in every one of them. He was always up for new experiences and challenges. "Glen is the master of moving goalposts," a friend observed. "His problem isn't that he doesn't have goals. His problem is that he has a hundred goals."

Still, he hadn't made any serious moves or given any real indication that a career change was in the offing.

At that surprise party, I got to meet Glen's siblings, Greg and Kate, for the first time. Glen had always talked about them so fondly that it felt as if I already knew them. Greg had written a speech for the event, which he and Kate delivered. They described a line in that magnificent Robert Redford film *A River Runs Through It*, where the older brother is recalling his father's struggle to find more memories of his younger son, Paul, the Brad Pitt character:

> As time passed, my father struggled for more to hold on to, asking me again and again: had I told him everything. And finally I said to him, "Maybe all I know about Paul is that he was a fine fisherman."
>
> "You know more than that," my father said. "He was beautiful." And that was the last time we spoke of my brother's death.

Greg likened Glen to the Brad Pitt character and said, "So we will tell you now, while you are still here, that you are beautiful."

During the party Greg pulled me aside and said, "Hey, Glen's doing some pretty heavy shit out there. I'm worried about him. Tell me he's going to be okay."

"He's solid," I assured him. "Glen has his act together, and it's a good outfit he's with. I don't think you have anything to worry about." Now I wish I could bury those words in the deepest mineshaft.

Arab Spring was five months away.

On June 19, 2012, not long after returning from Africa, Glen was hit by a car while riding his road bike—a nearly exact replay, strangely enough, of an accident that had injured Sonja five years earlier while they were going through their divorce.

The event seemed almost designed to put Glen out of commission. Not kill him or injure him badly, just take him out of circulation. The impact broke one arm, and the resulting fall badly injured his back, one knee, one wrist, and both elbows. Any normal person would have been laid up for a few months. But this was not any normal person. This was Glen. It barely slowed him down.

The next day he reported on e-mail:

> Got hit by a car riding my bicycle yesterday. Loopy on pain meds and typing with one hand so will be off the grid for a day or two. Could have been way worse. Only broken arm, jacked back/knee/elbows/wrist.

As the weeks wore on, he grew more and more frustrated at how long it was taking to recover. He wanted to get back into the action. In order to go back to Africa, he would have to take a fairly rigorous recertification process security agents are required to undergo every few years, which involved a physical test and a shooting test. He taped up his damaged arm, went in, and aced the test.

At lunch one day with me and another friend from the teams, Glen told us he was headed to Africa, then added, "This is my last run."

He'd been saying that for years, but it was finally starting to sound like he meant it.

We were working with two editor friends on a new edition of our book, and on August 17 Glen e-mailed us to cheer our progress:

> Very happy with the way all has been going. I don't know how to say thank-you enough. Healing has been slow, probably cause I'm so fucking OLD! Frustrating. Really frustrating. BUT, could have been way worse, and I'm go-

ing to Africa in three weeks, injured or no. I'll look forward
to when we can all get together and toast the new opus.

On September 5, Glen and I talked on the phone, figuring
we wouldn't get the chance again for a while, since he was
heading over to Africa the next day. We talked about him
coming to team up with me at SOFREP, which by this time
was soaring.

"You're a damn good writer, Bub," I said. "And there's no
one I trust more. You know how well you and I work together. I know this thing is a winner, and I really want you to
be a part of it."

Shooter and spotter. We'd always made an unstoppable
team, and we both knew it.

"We'll talk when I get back," Glen said.

Even with all the options he'd been looking at, especially
over the past few months, I'm not convinced that letting go
of his sheepdog duties and *not* going to Libya was ever really
on the table.

Tucking in hours when he could find them to work on
edits on our book, he e-mailed again a few days later:

I am fighting my way through the manuscript . . . finding
stuff to fix, little things here and there. Should be done by
the end of the weekend.

Hope all is well.
Best, Glen

On September 11, while Ambassador Chris Stephens's
compound in Benghazi was being attacked, Glen was safe and

sound in Tripoli, about six hundred miles to the west. When they got the news of what was going down, he and a fellow agent instantly knew they had to go help. Two Special Operations soldiers and a few case officers joined them. Told there were no flights available, they hit the airport anyway and managed to find a plane and a pilot who would get them over there immediately.

By the time they arrived in Benghazi, Stephens and defense attaché Sean Smith had both died, and the hostilities had migrated to the CIA compound in Benghazi. Glen and the others arrived at the place and Glen ran straight up to the roof, where the firefight was at its most intense. Reaching the roof, he saw Ty Woods, an agent he knew who was already at the CIA compound there. The two friends high-fived, and Ty yelled to the others, "Hey, guys, this is *Bub*!"

Everyone's best friend.

Within minutes mortar rockets had taken them both.

In an interview, Kate described her first moments after hearing the initial vague reports of trouble in Libya.

I was home with my three children when my brother's best friend [Sean] called me, concerned: Glen was in Libya, working as a security contractor, and he may have been at the U.S. consulate that had come under attack.

My first instinct was not to panic: I was used to his being in dangerous corners of the world—in and out of Iraq, Afghanistan, Mexico City—and he had always come home. His friend and I told each other not to worry. We agreed to talk again as soon as we knew anything.

I got on my computer and sent Glen an e-mail. "I'm worried," I said. "You better e-mail me this very second." I started pacing around the house. Then I called a friend and told her, "What I need you to tell me right now is not to worry—it will all be fine." And that's what she did. I wanted to hear that and I believed it. Glen was so larger-than-life, so smart, so good. He would be fine.

When the news first broke that something bad had happened in Benghazi, a handful of us started shooting e-mails back and forth to see who knew what. There were still no details. I hit "reply all" and wrote, "He's not on the state security detail, so don't take this as gospel, but it's probably not him." Then I boarded a plane from New York to San Diego.

The moment we landed in California I called one of my CIA buddies just to make sure. He didn't pick up, but he texted me back immediately:

Bad news.

A minute later he called me. The family hadn't been notified yet, he said. It was a short call.

I took a breath and called Sean, Glen's childhood friend. After all these years, they were still rooming together. I'd rather have him hear it from me. Got him on the first try. He didn't want to believe me at first, but he could tell from my voice that this was for real.

After we hung up, I sat in the parking lot of the San Diego airport and cried like a girl for fifteen minutes.

. . .

On September 20, I made the flight from the East Coast back to San Diego once again, this time on my way home from Glen's memorial service.

The night before the service they held a wake. Thousands of people showed up, and they finally had to turn people away as it poured rain. It felt like the whole state had turned out to mourn Glen, and even the clouds had joined in.

When Mike Bearden fell from the sky in 2000, I'd been out of town and didn't even find out until weeks after the service. When Dave Scott and Matt Axelson and John Zinn and all the other friends I lost over that decade perished, I still had not gone to a single memorial.

This time I went. It was impossible not to.

Now, twenty thousand feet over the heartland somewhere, I wrote the following words, my own memorial to Glen, which appeared the next day in full in the *New York Times*:

> Glen,
>
> I still can't believe you punched out early on me, but glad to hear from the guys that you fought like a hero—no surprise there.
>
> You should know, your efforts resulted in the rescue of over twenty Department of State personnel. They are alive today because of yours and Ty's heroic action.
>
> I know you hate funerals as much as I do, but the service in Winchester was humbling and inspiring. The people of Boston are amazing. I had to choke back the tears as me and

the boys rolled through town and thousands of people lined the streets to honor a hero and our friend and teammate. Seeing American citizens united around a hero, if only for a brief moment, restored my faith in humanity and that there are other things more important in life than killing each other.

Your family is and was amazing. Their poise, patience, and the dignity they displayed was incredible to witness. Your mom, Barbara, stood by stoically for hours to ensure she greeted everyone who came to pay their respects. She was an inspiration to everyone who watched. Seeing your dad, his sadness and how proud he was of you, made me give him a big hug, and reminded me to work harder at patching things up with my own father.

Greg delivered one of the best talks I've ever heard under the most difficult of situations. What an amazing brother; I hope to get to know him better. His speech made me reflect on my own life choices and how important our relationship with friends and family are. I'm going to work harder at embracing my friends and family the way you always did.

Katie gave such an awesome toast at the wake with all the Bub lessons to live by, I smirked secretly to myself knowing that I've heard them all before and will never forget. "Drive it like it's stolen!" and "Kids don't need store-bought toys; get them outdoors!" and all the rest.

Your nephews are amazing and so well behaved. Great parents, of course. FYI, I told them I'd take them flying when they come out west. They were beaming when I described all the crazy flying adventures me and their uncle went on. I told them how you and I would fly with my own kids and take turns letting them sit on our laps to get a few minutes at the controls. I'll do it up right and let them each have a go at the controls.

Sean has been steadfast in his support role and has handled everything thrown at him. Helping him this last week really showed me why he was such a close friend of yours. He's solid, and I look forward to his friendship for years to come. You chose well having him execute your will, he's solid.

We are all dedicated, as you explicitly indicated to us all, to throw you the biggest effing party we can, and to celebrate your life as well as our own. Done deal; Sean and I are on it.

Most of SEAL Team 3 Golf Platoon showed up in Boston. It was great to see how guys like Tommy B. just made stuff happen, no matter what was needed. Things just got handled like men of action handle them, no questions asked and no instructions needed—just get it done in true SEAL fashion.

One by one the Tridents were firmly pounded into the mahogany as the guys paid their respects. Mike and I handed the plank to your mom, choked back tears, and kissed her on the cheek. We both told her how much you'll be missed by us all.

Afterward, the Team guys, Elf, Steve, Sean and others tipped a few back in your honor. In good Irish fashion we drank whiskey from Sean's "What Jesus Wouldn't Do" flask, hugged each other like brothers and said goodbye, each in our own way.

We are planning the yearly surf trip to Baja in your memory. We share Steve Jobs's philosophy on religion and tolerance, but if you can arrange it, please talk to whomever and fire up a good south swell for me and the boys.

My kids will miss their Uncle Glen. I told them it's okay to cry (we all had a good one together) and to be sad but not for too long. You wouldn't want that. They will grow older and, like the rest of us, be better human beings for having known you.

You definitely lived up to the words of Hunter S. Thompson:

"Life should not be a journey to the grave with the intention of arriving safely in a pretty and well-preserved body, but rather to skid in broadside in a cloud of smoke, thoroughly used up, totally worn out, and loudly proclaiming 'Wow! What a ride!'"

When I skid in broadside in a cloud of smoke myself I'll expect to see your smiling face handing me a cold beer.

See you on the other side, brother. You are missed by many.

—B.W.

The thing I remember most about Glen was that he was happiest around a group of his close friends—and he redefined the meaning of the phrase "close friends." Most people go through life making friends along the way, but those friendships come and go. Not with Glen. He never let go of a friendship, ever. In his forties, he was still running around with the guys he knew when he was three.

The more I knew him, the more I realized that this wasn't something that just happened. He *worked* at it. "Friendship is like a garden," Glen told me once. "It needs attention if you want to maintain it and grow it." And Glen was a master gardener. He had a little black book he kept with him always, with probably several thousand names and numbers in it. Anytime he was sitting at the airport in between flights, or in a hotel stopover on a long trip, he would pull out the book and start going down the list, calling all his friends just to check in, say hi, and see how they were doing.

He taught me that true friendship is sacred, and that we should nourish it to the fullest extent possible.

No wonder thousands gathered at his memorial to celebrate his life and see him off to a better place.

There's one more thing you should know about Glen: He

specifically requested in his will that in the event of his death, there be no funeral held for him. He was quite explicit about it. Instead of a memorial, he wanted us to throw "a big fucking party." I laughed when I heard about that, and have since updated my own will to reflect the same request.

I knew we had to do the funeral anyway, for his family's sake and for the sake of the thousands of friends who showed up. There was no getting around it. But I knew secretly that Glen would be privately cursing us all.

Still, the fact that we held a memorial didn't mean we couldn't also give Glen that big fucking party he wanted. And that we did.

A few days after I got back to California, a throng of hundreds gathered on the beach in Encinitas and paddled out on surfboards. In the Hawaiian tradition of honoring a fallen friend or family member, flower leis were set adrift on the ocean. After a while we all repaired to the Del Mar Thoroughbred Club, which someone had donated for our venue. And it was a good thing we had a space that big, because people showed up from all over the world.

Glen himself had put it perfectly when he and his friends sat around a table for three in a tiny Filipino bar ten years earlier, almost to the day, grappling with the news of Dave Scott's death: "We all signed up for this. It's part of the fucking deal. So let's not sit here feeling sorry for him. Let's drink up and celebrate his life."

Among everyone who knew Glen, his death hit my children especially hard. They knew that I had lost different friends over the years—but their beloved uncle Glen? It didn't seem possible, and they were devastated. "It's okay to be sad," I told them, and we sat and cried together. But I also explained that we shouldn't feel sorry for Uncle Glen and others like him.

"Uncle Glen wouldn't want us to feel sorry for him," I said. "And here's the thing: He died living life to the fullest, doing what he absolutely loved, what he was passionate about."

How many of us can say that about our own lives?

It's so easy to sacrifice or marginalize our dreams, often for reasons that seem so important at the time but reveal their trivial nature when we look back years later. Glen never did that.

"Life goes by in a blink," I told my kids. "And here's something Uncle Glen taught us—you should each live your own lives doing what you love. Abandon your dreams for no one.

"That's the best way to honor Uncle Glen. Do your best to live the way he did."

On October 24, 2012, two of Glen's buddies and I took off from McClellan-Palomar Airport in the late afternoon in a little Piper Archer PA-28-180 I'd borrowed for the occasion. It was a clear, sunny day. Perfect. I piloted the plane down the coast at five hundred feet with a very slight tailwind, contacted San Diego International Airport over the La Jolla Cove, and requested a class B airspace clearance. Once through class B, I called the Navy tower at North Island and asked for a San Diego Bay arrival, bridge overfly, and clearance back up the coast by the Hotel Del Coronado and Point Loma at seven hundred feet.

We could hear the frustration in the controller's voice as he tried to brush us off. I didn't blame him: There were air ops ongoing in the area, and this was no time or place for some yahoos out for a joyride. But we were there on serious business, and once we explained our mission, the gent in the tower immediately granted us the access we needed. After holding over the Coronado Bridge for incoming H-60 helo traffic, we were cleared for a low flyby above the SEAL compound.

"Two minutes out," I signaled to my companions.

I pulled the throttle back gradually and put us into a slight descent to lose a few hundred feet, then trimmed and set power for a hundred feet over water right along the beach, as the main BUD/S compound came into view.

The sun was just starting to set over the distant Pacific horizon as we blazed past the obstacle course and watched a class of fresh SEAL candidates shuffling onto the asphalt grinder for some grueling evolution with their combat-seasoned SEAL instructors. A handful of students looked skyward as they jogged by, doubtless having no idea what we were doing there. All they would have seen was one lone guy propping open the door of the Piper and a slight puff of smoke disappearing behind us, as we let some of our friend's ashes loose over this place he held so dear.

See you on the other side, Glen.

CONCLUSION

One Saturday morning in early February 2013, I arrived at a gymnasium in Orange County to spend the day with some high school kids and their coaches. We were at a tournament, hosted by Nike, for the top-ranked high school basketball teams in the nation. A few former SEAL teammates and I had been invited to participate as part of a nonprofit initiative with my Red Circle Foundation and a twelve-year-old Virginia boy named Will Thomas.

When he heard the news about Extortion 17 being shot down back in 2011, Will was upset about it. He wanted to find a way to commemorate these guys and help their families, but had no idea how or even where to start. He decided he would build his project on something he loved and knew how to do: shoot baskets. Why not ask people to donate money for every basket he sank in these fallen heroes' honor? His father pledged a penny a basket, just to kick things off. Word spread. Within days he'd sunk twenty thousand baskets and raised fifty thousand dollars. Will decided to keep the effort going, and by early 2013 he had brought his total close to a hundred thousand dollars.

When Will and his dad invited me and the Red Circle Foundation to come out to the high school tournament and give some teamwork talks to the coaches and players there, I was more than happy to say yes.

The teams paired off and started playing their games. One by one, my two friends and I started giving talks to different groups as they cycled through the room that had been set aside for the purpose. It was a long day, and a gratifying one. These kids were very talented players. Many of them had full-ride scholarships to good colleges; a few were likely on their way to the NBA. And these weren't just top players; they were amazing kids: well behaved, sharp, respectful. When we got to the Q&A sessions they didn't ask the kinds of questions you expect from kids—"Was it hard to become a SEAL?" "What's it like to be a sniper?" "Did you ever kill anyone?" "What was the longest shot you ever took?"—and instead asked thoughtful questions about how they could become better players, how to foster stronger teamwork, and what were the most important elements to becoming excellent performers. It was impressive. These were some great coaches, and they weren't just coaching ball; they were teaching these teenagers how to become outstanding young men. For my two friends and me, it was a satisfying thing to see.

At the end of the day, after we'd given our last talk, Tony, the representative from Nike, came over to talk with me. "Hey, Brandon," he said, "there's one team we sponsored that didn't get a chance to hear from you yet, because their game is running late. You guys are supposed to be on your way home already. I don't want to impose. But they're a great group and their coach would really appreciate the chance for them to hear from you guys. Is there any way you'd be able to come over to their locker room and talk to them for a few minutes?"

"Of course," I said.

I walked with Tony to the gym where this group was playing and watched the end of the game, then waited while the team filed off into their locker room. I headed over there and stood outside the door for a moment. I was just about to open it and walk in when my phone buzzed. It was a text message from Melanie Luttrell, Marcus's wife:

Terrible news
Please call Marcus ASAP

A few seconds later I got a second text, this one from a SEAL buddy in Texas.

Chris Kyle has been shot to death in Texas.

My eyes closed and I felt myself slump against the wall. *Not again. Not another one. Not Chris.*

I gradually became aware of the muffled chorus of teenage voices, shouting and laughing and talking on the other side of the wall that was now holding me up. Young men in postgame locker room mode, exuberant, excited, their lives ahead of them. Waiting for me to come in and give them some inspiring words to end the day. Nobody else knew yet what had happened, not even my two SEAL buddies. How could I possibly face these kids? What could I tell them?

Someone else has got to do this, I thought. *Not me.*

. . .

I'd known Chris Kyle for more than a decade, but it was only in the last few years that we'd become friends as part of the small and tight-knit club of SEALs-turned-authors—which is less glamorous and a lot more problematic than it might sound. The common experiences that those of us in that group bond around have less to do with fame and media exposure and more to do with how much misunderstanding and heat we take from our own community.

There's a widespread sense in the Spec Ops community (though somewhat less so in the SEALs) that we are supposed to keep our mouths shut about everything pertaining to our service. It's like the first rule of Fight Club: *You do not talk about Fight Club.* But ever since September 11, 2001, the Naval Special Warfare (NSW) community has been propelled into the international spotlight by political grandstanding along with our own community's leadership, who have a long history of cooperating with Hollywood directors and celebrities. I believe the proximity of Coronado to Hollywood has probably played a significant role in all the attention. (Would you rather visit Fort Bragg in North Carolina or the Naval Amphibious Base in southern California? I rest my case.)

This newfound status is a media minefield. NSW is no longer a private community, and that is a painful reality for many of the guys I know or who have an association within the SEAL fraternity. It's a SEAL gold rush for journalists, the entertainment industry, the tactical industry, and others in a mad dash to cash in with no real regard for the community's long-term health and welfare.

Because of that new celebrity, it's even more crucial that SEALs examine how they conduct themselves in the public eye and on social media. An especially disturbing trend has been former operators violating the confidentiality/nondisclosure agreements associated with secret and top secret clearances. When guys cross this line they are not only breaking the law, they are also sacrificing their own integrity and hurting the community. "Will what I'm about to do reflect positively on the SEAL community?" is a mantra I carry with me at all times, and a question I ask before every media appearance. It's a question I think guys in the community need to take to heart.

I knew back in 2009 that the moment I appeared on CNN I would become a target for major criticism. I've been "read on" to confidential programs and it has always been crystal clear to me that these can never be discussed without approval through proper channels. I have always been 100 percent committed to keeping my integrity around protecting classified information I've been trusted with. Nevertheless, I knew that plenty of SEALs would peg me as selling out the Trident, some guy on an ego trip who violated the unwritten rule that Spec Ops guys stay out of the spotlight. I was prepared to deal with whatever bullshit or peer-group blowback followed, and despite the rocks that were hurled my way (yes, they came, and plenty of them), I had no regrets. I've never claimed to represent the entire SEAL community, but I have no problem contributing subject-matter expertise and weighing in on matters of national security and foreign policy, especially since running a media company has now become my second career. I'm incredibly proud of our veteran writing team at SOFREP.com. We've broken some big stories that the major media outlets couldn't touch (or were scared to), and the guys on the site do a tremendous job of keeping independent journalism and thought alive. I still contribute to the site often myself.

Like the decision to go public as a television news commentator, the decision to publish a book about my experiences was a choice made with the full understanding that I would catch some hell for doing it. We're not talking about mild, gentlemanly disapproval here. There are guys in the Spec Ops community who resent the hell out of the guys from Spec Ops—like Chris, Marcus, and me—who've had the audacity to publish memoirs.

So let's put the record straight on this one, right here and now: I don't apologize for a single word. In fact, I plan to keep writing. It's been highly therapeutic, my own PTSD drug of choice. And I'll take the side effects of writing over prescription drugs any day. I also think that those of us who have served have a perspective to offer that people won't get any other way. Special Operations is *not* Fight Club—it's an element of the United States Department of Defense. I think it's useful to give society a glimpse behind the Spec Ops curtain, not to disclose secrets but to convey a sense of who these sheepdogs are who give their lives protecting good citizens from the wolves of the world. And I think it's important that of all the books written about war and the Spec Ops community, at least a few are written by the people who have actually been there.

Of all the first-person SEAL accounts of the last few years, Marcus Luttrell's has by far been the most visible. What most people in the reading public don't realize is that Marcus has taken a *lot* of shit for writing *Lone Survivor*. What even fewer know—in fact, even most people in the Spec

Ops community, including 99 percent of his critics, don't know this—is that writing the damn thing in the first place was not Marcus's idea at all. The U.S. Navy *asked* him to write up his experiences into a book. He told me that, in fact, he was talked into it.

It's not hard to see why. For one thing, it's an incredible story, and it probably gave him much-needed closure to put it to paper. What's more, it's an even greater recruiting tool for the next generation of an all-volunteer active military. As I said, JT Tumilson's decision to become a SEAL came at age fifteen, when he read *Rogue Warrior*. Reading that same book was what solidified my own decision. For Dave Scott it was seeing the flick *Navy SEALs* at sixteen. How many kids are in the Special Operations pipeline right now because they were inspired by Marcus's story?

For me, the impulse to write *The Red Circle* came from watching Randy Pausch's "Last Lecture" video on YouTube and later reading his amazing book. I was moved by Professor Pausch's dedication to his family and the fact that he would pour so many of his precious last hours on earth into leaving a written record of what he'd learned about life for his three children. I had three children, too. Reading Pausch's book, I realized that I wanted them to know what their dad had gone through during those early years, what he was doing all that time he wasn't home with them, and why the sacrifices we all made mattered.

For Chris Kyle the situation was much as it was for Marcus: He had an amazing story that was begging to be told. At first, Chris told me, he was very resistant to the idea, but eventually he relented. "It got to the point where it was obvious somebody was going to write the damn thing," he told me. "I figured it might as well be me. Otherwise they'd probably just screw it up."

When his book *American Sniper* came out in January 2012, it became an instant sensation and has remained on the *New York Times* bestseller list ever since.

I saw him the following January at the 2013 SHOT Show in Vegas, where I introduced him to my good friend and fellow aviator Billy Tosheff. When I went up to Chris at the shooting range he gave me a big man-hug. I still have a picture of the two of us standing there together, that big goofy Texas grin on his face. You can see in the picture just how tall he is. I am not a short guy (five-ten), but standing next to Chris I look like a midget. As always, it was a blast to get together and spend a little time with him.

We never saw each other again.

Less than three weeks later I was standing slack against a high school gymnasium wall, gripping my iPhone and trying to grasp the news that Chris was gone, slain *by a suffering vet he was trying to help.* I tried to wrap my mind around that. I'm still trying.

Chris Kyle: another hero, another name etched onto my soul.

There is the unimaginable tragedy of those who never return from their service, men like Matt Axelson, Chris Campbell, Heath Robinson, and JT Tumilson, and the mothers and fathers, brothers and sisters, and children they leave behind.

Then there is the complicated toll it takes on those who *do* return.

For someone who's been in combat, everyday life in America, the life most of us take for granted as "normal," is a very strange world to come back to. The adrenaline of living on the edge becomes the new norm, and the men you serve with become your new adopted family. It's a hard thing to describe, but well portrayed by the Jeremy Renner character in the 2008 movie *The Hurt Locker* and his constant craving to be back in the *zone*.

I've been fortunate; in my case the transition to civilian life was not too difficult. I've been spared some of the uglier demons that can suck guys down the dark rabbit hole. I've seen the hell of addiction and how it can destroy good people, even on active duty. In my teens, when I was living on my own on the docks of southern California, I saw how easy it would be to turn to drugs, like some guys I ran with. By the time I was seventeen I knew I had to get out of there, which was in part what led me to the Navy. As I said, I was fortunate: That particular downward spiral never tugged at me too hard, not while on active duty or even after getting out of the service, something I probably owe in large part to having a circle of solid friends, my kids to anchor me, and mentors I could always talk to.

Still, I'm not the same person I was before I deployed to the Middle East in 2000 (USS *Cole*), Afghanistan in 2001 (SEAL Team Three Echo Platoon), and as a paramilitary contractor to Iraq in 2006.

None of us are.

The other day I was shopping at a little grocery store and noticed a guy cut rudely in front of an elderly lady as she stepped into the checkout line. I walked right up to him and said, "Hey, asshole, show a little courtesy." The other shoppers gaped at me, slack-jawed, and I could see them thinking, *Whoa, who is this guy?* and probably wondering whether maybe I was dangerous. I grant you, his was a minor offense, but I just don't have the patience for that kind of carelessness and lack of consideration. In Special Ops we're trained to have acute situational awareness at all times, which includes paying complete attention to whatever effect we might be having on those around us at every second. We can't turn that off. I know men who, rather than simply saying something to that rude line jumper, might have been tempted to grab him and yank him out of that line. Or worse.

I've said it twice now, but it's worth saying once more in conclusion: We are well into the longest continuous stretch of war in our nation's history. In 2012 we lost more guys to suicide than to combat. When you go to war for more than a decade, it has consequences. A lot of families have paid a terrible price for those consequences.

I took a deep breath and checked myself as I listened to the hum and buzz of the budding teen basketball stars on the other side of the wall. Tried to process what I'd just heard. I didn't know the details. All I knew was that Chris and a friend had both been found shot dead at a rifle range in Texas. The news hadn't hit the media yet, and nobody else in that locker room had any idea what had happened. They were all counting on me to go in there and give those young men an inspiring talk. So what now? What would Glen or any of my other fallen brothers want me to do?

I took another breath, opened the door, and walked into the locker room.

I don't remember exactly what I said. I know I talked about teamwork and sacrifice, and the fact that no matter who you are or how good you are at what you do, you can't accomplish anything truly worthwhile on your own. That any great achievement is always at its core a debt you owe to your teammates who hold you up and support you through the good times and bad.

And I talked about winning.

"We have a saying in the SEALs: 'It pays to be a winner.' I know you guys are all serious about being winners and being part of a winning team. So I'm not going to blow smoke about what that really means. Because winning is hard, and it takes more courage than most people know. Winning isn't about being lucky, or fortune smiling on you from above, or being graced with special talents. Winning is something you *decide* on, something that comes from the inside.

"You may have heard it said that winning is about refusing to accept defeat. Not true. That's just denial.

"You can't avoid failing. You're *going* to fail. The question is, How will you deal with failure? Because what you do next will make the difference between ultimate failure or success in the long term. Sometimes losing is what helps motivate you to win.

"The truth is, winners are the ones who understand loss, who understand adversity and hard work and don't run from any of it. One individual can affect the whole team with how he chooses to deal with a tough break." (*Or heartbreak,* I thought but didn't say.) "Winners play full-out and refuse to give in, no matter what. Loss hurts, and it's part of the game. Accept it, embrace it, use it as your teacher. 'I will never quit,' the Navy SEAL creed says. 'I persevere and thrive on adversity. If knocked down, I will get back up, every time.'"

At least, that's what I think I said. My fellow SEAL teammate Mark Donald was there and spoke some great words of his own. Tony told me afterward it was the best talk we gave all day. I was just glad I made it through.

Three months later, on Mother's Day 2013, Donna Axelson's phone rang. It was Ben Foster, the actor who was playing her son, Matt, in the forthcoming film version of *Lone Survivor*.

Donna and her husband, Corky, had spent quite a bit of time with Ben as he prepared for the role, talking with him about Matt. So had Cindy, Matt's widow. Marcus put in probably the most time of all, making sure Ben had a complete understanding of who Matt was. Which is probably a big part of the reason Foster does such an amazing job. When I first saw the finished film, I could have sworn I was watching actual footage of Matthew. It's uncanny.

Most Hollywood films about SEALs aren't worth the price of the popcorn. *Lone Survivor* is a rare exception to that rule. First time I saw the trailer, I was stunned and wept silent tears. My date was with me and asked me what was wrong. "Give me a moment here," I said, and let the tears fall, realizing how fortunate I was to still be here and be able to hug my kids at night. Peter Berg, the director, did an excellent and respectful job. So did the actors, who put in days and days at a range with live ammo, being schooled by active-duty frogmen in how to handle their weapons correctly and get it all right. They had a strong incentive to get it all right: Marcus met with the film's key creative team in a boardroom, early on in the process, and told them, "If you fuck this up, I'll kill you all." Of course, they knew he was kidding. (Right, Marcus?)

By May 2013, though, all this was in the past, and shooting for the film had long since wrapped. So why was Foster calling Donna now?

Just to call and talk.

"Happy Mother's Day, Donna," he said. "I just wanted to call to tell you what a great mother you are."

The following month, on Matt's birthday, he called her again. Just to talk.

What I love so much about this story is that what Foster was doing, and what Peter Berg and his team have accomplished, serves to keep Matt Axelson alive. Most of us don't have at our disposal the multimillion-dollar storytelling resources of a Hollywood studio to give these memories flesh and breath. The best we can do is just to keep telling one another the stories.

My generation of SEALs has seen at least fifty of its members killed in Iraq and Afghanistan, more than any other generation of frogmen before us. I still struggle to explain how this has affected me and those of us who knew them. Over the decade I was part of the SEAL teams I made some of the closest friends I've ever had. Think about half a dozen of your closest friends—and then imagine that a year or two from now they are all suddenly gone.

"For the first year after losing Dave," Jack Scott said recently, "we didn't go a minute without thinking about him. It was like having a hole broken in a pane of glass—a hole in your reality that you can't even get close enough to touch without being cut by its sharp edges. Those edges are gradually worn a little smoother by the passage of time; more than a decade later, we don't get cut so easily. But it's still a hole, and it always will be."

I've written this book in part to help soften those razor edges, both for myself and for the Scotts, the Beardens, the Axelsons, the Zinns, the Dohertys, and all the other family members who have had their sons, brothers, husbands, and fathers taken away.

In larger part, though, my goal in telling these stories is to celebrate the value of what's been *added* to our lives, to *my* life, by passing on the lessons these men have left behind.

After reviewing this manuscript, Glen's brother, Greg, e-mailed us. "I'm grateful to hear the stories," he wrote. "Hearing his voice really brings him back." That's exactly why I often find myself rereading saved e-mails from these men. Greg put it perfectly: Hearing their voices *brings them back*. They are voices I don't want to forget, because they still have so much to say.

Mike Bearden showed me what it means to devote yourself with all your heart to the safety and well-being of others. He was a watchful, protective big brother to everyone who knew him. I will never forget him.

Dave Scott made me laugh one minute and gasp in amazement the next. His mind traveled faster and farther than anyone else's I've known. Rapier-tongued and kindhearted, he pushed every envelope he could find and showed me that your only limitations are those you choose to accept for yourself. I will never forget him.

Matt Axelson inspired everyone with whom he came into contact with his unshakable dedication to excellence and his stoic nature. He saw only the best in others, and was fiercely committed to only the best in himself. I will never forget him.

John Zinn showed me how to pull something that doesn't exist yet out of the ether of imagination and make it into reality. He also showed me that it *is* possible to pursue outstanding professional achievement and have a fulfilling, consistent family life at the same time. I will never forget him.

Chris Campbell taught me that life is what you make of it, regardless of how terrible the situation gets; that we are the ones who control our own environment, and not vice versa. I can still see his big shit-eating grin beaming at me as we sit frozen, up to our necks in ice-cold water, in that damn rinse tank. I will never forget him.

Heath Robinson's enthusiasm for life, quest for achievement, and deep love of America made me a better person for knowing him. He made the world a safer place for those I love. I will never forget him.

JT Tumilson showed me that becoming the best of the best doesn't mean setting aside your humanity—that it is, in fact, an expression of that humanity. I will never forget him.

Glen Doherty showed me what it means to love life and live it full-out, to spend every moment in a sense of exhilaration at the privilege of simply being here on this planet. His unfailing dedication to an ever-expanding sphere of close friends was an inspiration to me, as it was to the thousands who knew him. I am a better friend, son, and father because of him. I will never forget him.

Chris Kyle was a warrior in the best and noblest sense, a bare-knuckle Texan and champion of the no-bullshit truth who had no hesitation putting his life on the line for his brothers, and I will never forget him.

"Don't worry about me; I'm doing great here," JT Tumilson told his mom, Kathy, shortly after arriving in Afghanistan in the summer of 2011. "Listen," he added, "if I die, at least I die doing something I love."

Every one of these heroes felt exactly the same way.

"They weren't heroes to themselves," says Kathy. "They were just doing what needed to be done, because they loved people and wanted to keep them safe." To me, that's what makes them heroes.

I will never forget any of them—and I hope you don't either.

Share their stories with your friends, your family, the people you love. Keep their memories alive and learn from them, as I have and continue to do. If you want to honor them, emulate them. As I told my kids when they were heartbroken over Glen's death: "That's the best way to honor Uncle Glen. Do your best to live the way he did."

Knowing these men has made my life immeasurably richer. I hope it does the same for you.

AFTERWORD

THE RED CIRCLE FOUNDATION

One way to honor the memories of our fallen heroes is to help their families, who are often afflicted with grievous financial burdens along with their grief.

"I still remember getting that phone call," says Jackie Zinn, John Zinn's widow. "They told me my husband was dead. And the second thing they told me was that it was going to cost me twenty thousand dollars to get his body back home."

When my friend Glen died in the September 11, 2012, attack in Benghazi, his name was in the news for weeks, along with the names of Ty Woods, Chris Stevens, and Sean Smith. Their memories were evoked and paraded across the stage in political speech after political speech. Then over time the inevitable appetite of that hungry monster, the news cycle, needed fresh feeding, and their names slowly slipped out of sight. And then what?

As of this writing, more than a year later, Glen's family still has not received a penny of death benefit or assistance from the government. We're not talking about some big payoff here; we're talking about the basic costs of burying someone properly and holding a memorial service for those who gathered to honor him. Hasn't happened. After Glen's nearly two decades of service to his country, his family was left not only to bury their dead, but to do so out of their own pockets. The Dohertys' experience is far from unique.

This is what those of us who have served in the military call UNSAT: decidedly, emphatically *un*satisfactory.

Fortunately there is a wide range of military charities and other private nonprofit organizations that pick up some of the slack. This is one of the great things about America: Say what you will about the problems in our country, we do have a powerful ethic of taking care of our own.

At the same time, the charities are not without their own problems, including abuse of funds and undue influence of self-interest among their administrators. As with political organizations, scratch the surface and it's not unusual to find people lining their own nests instead of taking care of the people they were empowered to help. Don't get me wrong: There are many organizations that do a tremendous amount of good works. But it's important to do your due diligence before giving them your hard-earned dollars.

Starting in 2012 I had a problem: I was starting to have some professional success, and I wanted to begin channeling some of the profits from those achievements into supporting the families of Spec Ops heroes who'd given their lives to protect us all. But I also wanted to know exactly where that money was going.

In the teams we had a principle drilled into us from day one: Never complain about a problem unless you have a solid solution. My solution to that problem was to start my own foundation. In the spring of 2012, the Red Circle Foundation opened its doors.

At first our mission was broad and somewhat vague. As we began collecting contributions, we knew we were going to support the families of the Spec Ops community, but hadn't worked out yet exactly how. The answer wasn't long in coming.

When Glen died in September, our mission suddenly gained a very personal focus. When I saw how Glen's family was left hanging with their memorial expenses, and how stressed it made them to have to deal with this financial burden on top of the deep wounds of personal loss, the foundation's existence suddenly became very real. We made our first payout to the Doherty family for about eleven thousand dollars. It didn't cover everything by any stretch, but it sure helped. I'll never forget how great it felt to cut that check.

The Red Circle Foundation is what we in the military call a QRF—a quick reaction force. When these families are hit with memorial costs or emergency medical expenses, they are hit suddenly and hit hard. While private organizations typically have nothing like the bureaucracy of a Veterans Administration, which can be maddeningly byzantine, they can still move way too slowly. It can take weeks to months before funds are deployed to help people in need. This is where the RCF comes in. We can make decisions in hours and provide immediate assistance to bridge the gap, and in the process make a huge difference in people's lives. The RCF also provides scholarship funds to send children of Spec Ops parents to schools, camps, and other enrichment programs.

Because the foundation is personal to me, involving my

own assets in some cases and putting my own reputation on the line in every case, I needed someone I could trust unequivocally to run it, and who would be in a position to step in and make a full-time commitment. That person turned out to be my sister, Maryke, who was then working for a major U.S. airline carrier. Starting as part-time executive director at the foundation, she was able to phase out her airline work and eventually make her position at RCF full-time.

Not long after she started, Maryke came to me with an idea. She told me about an organization that works to bring clean, safe drinking water to people around the world. "I really like what they're doing," said Maryke. Not only were they doing good in the world; they were running their operation on what they call the 100% Model, which meant that they relied on private sponsors and corporate donors for all their operating expenses and channeled every penny of general contributions to the projects themselves.

I loved the idea. It would put to rest any doubts or concerns about where people's money is going, because it's black-and-white: 100 percent means 100 percent.

We made it our goal to adopt the same model. In the summer of 2013 we held our first annual gala fund-raiser to generate as much money as we could to help meet operating costs, and we continue to hold a gala every year at the New York Athletic Club. Corporate donors cover the rest of our overhead. Which means that if you give thirty dollars or thirty thousand dollars, you know that every penny of that money is going directly to a military family who needs it. Period. As of this writing, we may be the only military charity that does this.

I've gone into this brief history of our foundation for a

simple reason. I want to close this account of heroes I've known with a request: If you've learned from them, if knowing about their lives has served to enrich your own, then deepen that bond by giving financially to help ease the burden on their families.

You don't have to be wealthy or give large amounts for it to be genuinely meaningful. Even the smallest donations can make a difference. (Will Thomas started with a penny, and look where *that* went.) It doesn't matter whether you help through our own Red Circle Foundation or one of the other trusted charities set up to assist the families of fallen heroes—provided you do your due diligence and make sure your contributions go where you mean them to go.

My hope for this book is that these men become in some small way a part of your life. And through a simple act of generosity, you can become part of theirs.

GRATITUDE

Instinctively I knew this was a story that needed to be told, but the telling proved to be more challenging than I expected. Writing is normally a fairly straightforward process for me; a story wants out, and it pours itself onto the page. Not so with this book. It was surprisingly tough to work out just how to shape my experiences and memories of these great men into a positive narrative that others could learn from and take inspiration from, and not simply a chronicle of tragedy and loss. My writing partner, John David Mann, and I anguished for months over the best way to proceed. John, I'm forever in your debt for sticking with me during this difficult journey. It was worth it!

John and I also owe a huge thank-you to Brent Howard, our editor at New American Library. You went out on a limb for us after our manuscript had a rough start. Your support, thinking, and contribution have been extremely valuable, and we have a better book because of it. Our thanks also to Kara Welsh, our publisher, for believing so strongly in this book; to Pete Garceau for that incredibly powerful cover design; to copy editor Tiffany Yates, for your perceptive and sensitive touch; and to Christina Brower, for too many assists to count. And another huge thank-you to our literary agent, Margret McBride, for connecting us in the first place and seeing this project through.

This book is dedicated to the families who raised the remarkable men described in these pages. It was your love and unwavering support that forged these modern-day American heroes. You stood ready to give your all, and did so bravely, proudly, and without bitterness, despite the depth of your losses. John and I especially want to thank those family members who graciously shared your time and memories with us, willingly opening old wounds and sharing your private pain so that we could bring these stories to life. (Fortunately that pain is intermingled with lasting joy, love, and hilarity; there were plenty of laughs mixed in with the tears in those interviews.) Thank you to Michael and Peggy Bearden, Wendy Bearden, Derenda Fugate, Jack and Maggie Scott, Kat Colvert, Donna Axelson, Cindy Oji, Michael Zinn and Jackie Zinn, Cindy Campbell, Debora Coxe, Kathy Tumilson, Joy (née Tumilson) McMeekan, Kate (née Doherty) Quigley, Greg Doherty, and Barbara Doherty.

And thank you to the friends and teammates who did the same, climbing on the phone in the midst of hectic schedules to help us bring these memories to life: Walt Anderson, DeVere Crooks, Eric Davis, Elf Ellefson, Josh Emrick, Dave Fernandez, Lee Ferran, Ron Griffin, Randy Kelley, Sean Lake, Travis Lively, Mike Ritland, Dave Rutherford, and Clint Smith.

I also want to thank my own family for their unwavering support in this process: Thank you to my mother, Lynn, for your honesty and incredible support. Thank you to my father, Jack; you were a major influence in my decision to enlist in the Navy and, ultimately, to join the SEALs. Thank you to my sister, Maryke, for agreeing to take on the major task of running the Red Circle Foundation. I had no idea how tough the nonprofit world is. It's such a relief to be able to trust someone so completely to always do the right thing, no matter what the situation.

Thank you to my incredible children, who continue to amaze me every day. Not a day goes by that I don't think of the three of you and of how lucky I am to be present in your lives. You may not know it yet, but you serve as my inspiration to improve myself and push beyond what I think is possible in my own life.

Finally, my never-ending thanks to Mike Bearden, Dave Scott, Matt Axelson, John Zinn, Chris Campbell, Heath Robinson, JT Tumilson, Glen Doherty, Chris Kyle, and the many other brothers not written about here who likewise laid down your lives so that the rest of us might sleep more peacefully in our beds at night. You are sorely missed, but never forgotten.

To borrow that once again from the late, great Hunter S. Thompson: "Life should not be a journey to the grave with the intention of arriving safely in a pretty and well-preserved body, but rather to skid in broadside in a cloud of smoke, thoroughly used up, totally worn-out, and loudly proclaiming 'Wow! What a ride!'"

When I skid in broadside in a cloud of smoke myself, I look forward to seeing *all* your smiling faces.

See you all on the other side, gents.

Courtesy of Brandon Webb

BRANDON WEBB is the *New York Times* bestselling author of *The Red Circle* and *Benghazi: The Definitive Report*. A former U.S. Navy SEAL whose last assignment was course manager for the elite SEAL sniper course, he was instrumental in developing new curricula that trained some of the most accomplished snipers of the twenty-first century. Webb has received numerous distinguished service awards, including the Presidential Unit Citation. As CEO of Force12 Media and editor of SpecialOperations.com, he runs the largest military content network on the Internet.

JOHN DAVID MANN, who collaborated with Webb in writing *The Red Circle*, is an award-winning author whose titles include the *New York Times* bestseller *Flash Foresight* and the international bestseller *The Go-Giver*.

CONNECT ONLINE

brandontylerwebb.com